MW00596848

"I meet countless patients who are tackling the emotional and mental hurdles that come with a blood cancer diagnosis and treatment. When I met Bishoy and heard his inspiring story in 2017 at our National Blood Cancer Conference in New York City, I was struck by his determination not only to survive his cancer but to 'dare' himself and those around him to adopt a mindset of breaking barriers. Bishoy's commitment to LLS is having a profound impact on our ability to invest in new and better treatments for cancer patients."

—Dr. Louis DeGennaro, President and CEO,
The Leukemia and Lymphoma Society

"As I've told Bishoy, 'Victim or life lesson. It's a choice and it's yours to make.' Chances and choices are what we are given everyday. The decisions we make about them are what define the outcome of life's journey. I am happy that Bishoy chose to be better every day."

—Eugene Alletto, CEO, Bedgear

"I've heard Bishoy tell his story in person and even ran part of the New York City Marathon with him! It's not just a story of running — his journey is comparable to the race of life. Rather than dreaded miles, his challenges became building blocks! His determination is inspirational for anyone staring down any obstacle."

—Amy Freeze, Running Reporter, WABC-TV,
and nine-time Marathoner

# BREAK BARRIERS

**How Setbacks Can Dare You**

**Rather than Define You**

BISHOY TADROS

© Bishoy Tadros, 2019
All rights reserved

Tadros, Bishoy.
Break barriers : how setbacks can dare you rather than define you.
ISBN 9781086196627

Printed in the United States of America
Set in Minion and Myriad Pro
Designed by Fredrick Haugen

This book is sold subject to the condition that it shall not, by way of trade or otherwise, be lent, resold, hired out, or otherwise circulated without the publisher's prior consent in any form of binding or cover other than that in which it is published and without a similar condition including this condition being imposed on the subsequent purchaser.

The scanning, uploading, and distribution of this book via the internet or via any other means without the permission of the publisher is illegal and punishable by law. Please purchase only authorized electronic editions and do not participate in or encourage electronic piracy of copyrightable materials. Your support of the author's rights is appreciated.

To Mom & Dad, and Vina

# Contents

# Foreword

## by Michael Capiraso
## President & CEO, New York Road Runners

What inspires you? More specifically, what inspires you to run? What catalyst sparked something in you to channel your energy, strife, and hardship into motivation? Some run for health, some run to overcome, some do it in memory of a loss, and others to inspire the next generation. Running can be a connector, an escape, a way to prove something to the world or to yourself.

I'll never forget the feeling of running my first New York City Marathon. It was 1991 and, after some unexpected life changes, I impulsively registered to run as an attempt to steer myself back on course. Upon hitting that finish line in Central Park, I discovered a new passion, a journey of renewed inspiration. The impact of that decision has been lifelong. It brought me to a sport and lifestyle that has forever changed me: personally, professionally, and physically.

Years along this adventure, I've found myself lucky enough to experience both sides of the finish line: crossing it multiple times as a runner as well as greeting thousands of finishers as the President and CEO of New York Road Runners.

As much emotional satisfaction as I've experienced personally from the feat of 26.2 miles, nothing can compare to experiencing the magnitude of the Marathon by witnessing thousands of runners pour over that finish line. To be a part of the immeasurable impact produced by the New York City Marathon is an embarrassment of riches and not something I take for granted.

Among the sea of inspiration, I've had the chance to connect with individual marathoners, to hear each one's incredible story: the catalyst for taking this life-altering journey and the challenges and triumphs to bring them to the starting line. One of the runners that stands out to me is Bishoy.

I met him prior to the 2017 TCS New York City Marathon. It was Bishoy's first time, and he was raising money for The Leukemia and Lymphoma Society following his childhood battle with leukemia. I found him, then and now, to be exceptionally humble and engaging. I'm inspired by his motivation to take on new challenges, to work towards achieving a goal—to break barriers.

Bishoy joined us at our annual New York Road Runners Charity Partner Forum to share his story and speak to his fundraising efforts. He not only uses his life experience to give back, but inspires others to do the same. Paying it forward is one of the many things that makes Bishoy, and his story so moving and motivating.

That halo effect of inspiration is what makes the New York City Marathon so unique and compelling. The event creates a platform to share these stories and reach countless others. Collectively, we can harness the Marathon to touch thousands of lives.

*Break Barriers* brings readers into the physical, emotional, and mental aspects of running a marathon. It's measured not just by each step through the five boroughs on race day, but by sacrifice and dedication over the months of training leading up to the event.

Crossing that line is a culmination of a tremendous amount of hard work that often goes unseen or untold. For Bishoy, the 26.2-mile journey was a lifetime in the making. I'm so excited for his story to be shared here.

# Preface

A personal journey may not be fully understood in the present, yet it should be embraced, since we have limited control of the future. It took me thirty years to accept my mantra: Break Barriers. As I go through life, I continue to square up against obstacles head-on without hesitation. I trust that I can overcome any barrier.

You might wonder from where this confidence arises? Well, that's the purpose of this book: to walk you through how I tried and tested my mantra. To put it simply, barriers are meant to be broken. If you embrace the mindset that obstacles appear in your life to *dare* you rather than *define* you, you are taking the first and most important step in unleashing your highest potential.

When you understand that the moments which have the power to break you are, in fact, the same moments that highlight your strength, then you can access the depth of your potential whether it's inside the classroom or the boardroom, on the playing field or over the dinner table. I know that, in due time, I can overcome any barrier, no matter how insurmountable. And so can you.

# BREAK BARRIERS

# When Strength Was the Only Option

# 1

# City of Hope

On Saturday mornings, you couldn't drag me away from the TV. The cartoons were on and already, at the ripe old age of four, I had my rituals. Hours of animated entertainment was one of them.

In that way and others, I was like any other kid my age: curious, full of questions, and maybe a tad bit whiny. I was always eager to run outside and play in the shimmer of the southern California sun. Happy to come back inside to the embrace of my mother and the fragrant scent of boiling cabbage. Stuffed cabbage, an Egyptian delicacy, was my favorite food.

It was Los Angeles, 1991. North of there in the ample green meadows of Arcadia—a small city situated near the base of the San Gabriel Mountains. I wasn't aware of it at the time, but my parents had chosen this community expressly for me. Besides the beautiful setting and safe neighborhoods, there was an excellent school system awaiting. But, most importantly, Arcadia was near City of Hope and the doctors there. The same doctors who told my parents that I had a huge mountain to climb, larger than the San Gabriels.

Children are infinitely adaptable to their circumstances. What you experience is what you know. It's all you know; no matter what that might entail. It's your version of average: the baseline, the place from which you measure.

I was unaware of what I was battling in terms of treatment. I didn't comprehend the severity of my initial diagnosis. I never felt like there was a vast mountain to climb as my doctors suggested, and I took each day as it came my way.

I had been through more procedures and seen more needles than most children; however, I had no gauge of pain; as far as I could tell, everything I had lived through was normal.

The City of Hope was recognized for its highly–touted cancer treatment program, and in my eyes as a young child, it was a happy place. I had no idea what cancer was; I was unaware of all the heart–wrenching stories and the plights other families went through. I was playing with Lego sets; I was being catered to by the nurses; I was a VIP in the playrooms.

The City of Hope didn't feel like a hospital; it felt like a privilege for me. I was excited to go there; it had that field trip feeling. Nights spent hooked up to IV's were pleasant, the atmosphere was overly hospitable, and the staff felt like family.

Then came that terrible day, the day I never saw coming, and one that I'll always remember. My father knew what lay ahead; my mother had educated herself with all of the resources that were provided to her, yet she couldn't fully gauge what was to occur.

I was taken into my doctor's office, and per usual as soon as I got on the examination table, all of the paper scrunched up, I was very fidgety. The doctor asked the typical questions like any other check–up, and my father answered him. To my mind, it seemed like business as usual.

The doctor then proceeded to let my dad know that he'd probably need to hold on to me tightly. He asked me to lie down on my stomach. "Don't worry," Dad said. "Everything is going to be okay. Just listen."

Before I could process what was happening, I thought I felt the sting of a painful death. It was my first spinal tap, the needle went straight into my spine, and the scream was deafening. Before that moment, I had never encountered a sensation so shattering. Never before that did I feel my body could be physically torn in half.

That day is forever engrained with me: the off-white paint on the walls, the bright lights contrasted against the darkness of my screams, the compassion of the doctor who was just doing his job, and the pain in my father's eyes as he watched helplessly. I had met my highest known level of distress, physically and mentally.

I could not imagine living through more considerable pain, and I certainly could not rationalize what I had done to deserve it. It felt like a punishment for a crime that was not committed.

All I knew was that I never wanted to go back. I had to go every six months or so, and the experience never got better, my father dreaded those days, strategizing different positions to hold me down to hopefully alleviate some of the pain.

*

During my early years of treatment at the City of Hope, I began to recognize that I was different. If not for anything, none of the kids that I had been engaging with at that time had been talking about how their parents took them to that dreaded room, so I quickly picked up that it was just me and I was alone in experiencing that sting at the hands of my doctor.

I couldn't justify it, and it scared me to my core anytime that I found out that we were going back; the screams began from the moment we'd get in the car. Those experiences were personal; they were intimate and dark. After leaving the room, my parents and I didn't speak about it—my pain was compartmentalized to that room. I was building up a sense of awareness, and also insecurity.

At the age of four, there is nothing worse than the feeling of being left out, and that rings even louder if you did nothing, in particular, to deserve that seclusion. Outside of begging my parents never to take me back to that room, I never spoke of my burden. The other children had no idea what I had been through; there were no visible marks or scars. Physically at that point in my life, I didn't look much different than your typical preschooler. I was able to hide my battle, and that gave me comfort.

I had grown accustomed to seeing multiple doctors at a time, listening to my dad as he answered all of their questions, I knew when the needles were coming and going, and I had my routine down for squeezing my fists ahead of time so they could find the vein to pop in the IVs.

This was the life I was living, and I didn't think much of it. The issue that snuck up on me, however, was that I was almost too comfortable and—due to the volume of injections—the doctors determined that I needed to have a tube inserted into my chest to facilitate all of the treatment.

If I didn't stand out before, I was going to stand out now. As they completed the procedure, I looked down at my chest: it was horrendous, like an elephant trunk sticking out. I knew I was going to have trouble explaining it to anyone that asked.

I had no idea why it was there, and I didn't know how long it was going to stay. Above all that, I had no understanding of the limitations that it would bring forth.

I couldn't run wild and free outside; I couldn't swim. I was restricted. Why was I the only one who had to go back to that room? Why was I the only one that couldn't play? It seemed like all the other kids were living their best tube-free lives.

I had to get these tubes inserted on more than one occasion: once through my neck and once through my chest. Those scars remain with me to this day. They are, in fact, the only physical reminders I have from my bout with cancer. It's funny how life works, those tubes were at one point my biggest physical insecurity, and now all I see is beauty in the most hideous accessory.

The tubes signify resilience and strength. The restriction they imposed not only tested me physically, but they tried me mentally and emotionally as well. I came to realize that I was not just an immigrant child assimilating to a new land, I was an immigrant cancer patient, and it showed.

*

Education is virtually everything when it comes to Egyptian society. Somehow every Egyptian parent was "the top of his/her class." I'm really not sure how that came to be the case. Egyptian communities across the world overflow with a multitude of successful professionals across industries.

Typically, all parents take pride in their children succeeding academically, and within my culture, that pride is amplified. From an early age, Egyptian parents stress the importance of schooling and try to instill a career path for their children.

In my particular case, my mom and dad were very aware of not losing track of my education in spite of managing my treatment, and being in a new country with a different schooling system. To provide me with the best learning environment, my parents were big believers in the Montessori system. They sought out the best preschool in Arcadia, and I was enrolled. They had every good intention for me, factoring all the reviews and doing all their homework when it came to academic reputation.

There is, however, one thing my parents did not consider: demographics. They were so focused on the learning experience that perhaps they forgot that—unlike in Egypt where everyone comes from the same background and speaks the same language—in this case, I was going to be the odd man out.

English was not my first language. My parents had started using it more in our house to help me pick things up. But, in spite of that, I was still speaking a mix of Arabic and English. They assumed that I'd pick up more English when I started engaging with classmates.

Unfortunately, that plan backfired.

The thing my parents didn't consider before enrollment was that Arcadia was home to a large Asian community. So, instead of picking up on English, I began regressing. While my classmates were speaking one language (Mandarin), I was now spouting a hodgepodge of three idioms—one of which, the most newly-acquired, I had no real understanding of.

Beyond language, I clearly did not look the same. I did not share the same interests as my classmates; I did not eat the same food. I had no means to relate to the other kids at all.

I found myself assessing my environment, thinking incessantly: How did I end up here? What did I do to deserve this? Do my parents have any idea where they are sending me every day?

I put no effort toward befriending classmates; I just wanted the experience to end. I couldn't imagine the rest of my life would be this alienating. Every day at pre-school I couldn't wait to get home.

Unbeknownst to me, my parents were planning our next move, so there was a light at the end of the tunnel. I wanted to eliminate that year from my memory. I thought to myself that, once I began kindergarten, things would make more sense.

My father, a priest in the Coptic Orthodox Church, had been called to serve on the other side of the continent—to a young church of about a hundred families on Long Island. Though I didn't know it at the time, Woodbury, New York, was a far cry from the suburbs of Los Angeles.

My family prepared for the move. Besides the usual things, there was the issue of my care. I was to transfer all my files and continue treatment at the North Shore University Hospital (now a part of NorthWell Health).

I never looked back on my time in California; I was ready for the next phase of my life. I was convinced that I could start anew someplace else. I was prepared to navigate a new environment, ready, above all else, to fit in and just be a kid.

## 2

# "We're in This Together"

It was August, 1986, in Heliopolis, a modern suburb outside of Cairo. The desert air abounded with the oppressive heat of summer. A 27-year-old physician sat alone in a room at his parents' home, thinking about his future. Having completed medical school only three years prior, he was in the early stages of a promising career.

The physician was the youngest of four children. As such, he had witnessed the others grow up and mature ahead of him. Each of his siblings led a successful life in their respective profession. They were starting their families and building their homes while he was still living at home.

His name was Sherif, and he was about to make the single most important decision of his life. After much deliberation, he decided to change the course of his entire career—to forsake the burgeoning medical practice that his father had helped him to set up.

Instead this handsome man with short dark hair and a full, but meticulously-trimmed, mustache chose to follow a calling from deep inside his soul into a life of pastoral service. He decided to become a priest in the Coptic Orthodox Church.

Sherif was uncertain if he could provide the capacity of service that would be required, unsure if the priesthood was the right call or if he should remain involved in the Church as a laymen. He only knew it was where he found fulfillment, so he had to see it through.

He was engaged at the time to a beautiful 22-year-old woman who had grown up with Sherif in the same community. Her name was Nancy. They had known each other as friends, so when he approached her regarding their courtship, there was little hesitation on her part despite the uncertainty that comes with being the wife of a priest. "We're in this together" was their commitment to each other, no matter what future sacrifice they would have to make.

Thus, a few short months after he made the choice to become a priest (though not one yet), Sherif wed his fiancé, Nancy. Now, in Egypt, the churches operate at all hours of the day, so functions such as weddings and baptisms occur practically around the clock, with crowds constantly coming and going. Their union was no different. Sherif and Nancy married in early November, to much buzz, surrounded by a multitude of friends and loved ones.

A few weeks after the couple returned from their honeymoon on the Red Sea coast, it was decided that Sherif would be ordained in his hometown. In the Coptic Orthodox Church, a priest changes his name upon ordination. Thus Sherif became known to the world as Father Guirguis (Guirguis being a variation of the patron saint George). For this story, I'll use the easier-to-pronounce name.

Though in the Catholic Church a priest takes a vow of celibacy, under Coptic Orthodox tradition, it is mandated that clergy enter into marriage. Culturally, a priest is held in high regard—almost like a figurehead shepherding a flock of thousands. As a result, the congregation is very active in selecting who will lead them.

Father George was particularly full of energy and, in Heliopolis, there was a highly-engaged group of his contemporaries. This group was compelled to find someone to lead them in matters of spiritual counseling; they wanted someone who could bridge the generational gap—someone who articulated a message of hope.

They handpicked Father George, and he accepted, all the while aware that his life was about to shift gears. Leading a congregation was not a decision to be taken lightly, but for him, there was an element that felt natural. He had grown up involved in serving his church community, and he had a knack for relating to the masses.

Frankly, the young Father was a charismatic speaker; he had a keen ability to simplify complex topics. Moreover, he thought of this life of service as an extension of serving patients as a physician.

Life was coming together. Father George began his service in the bustling city. As a gift, his father had purchased an apartment— a modest place that the couple moved into. Nancy started to set up the home, and explored prospective career opportunities. Things were moving at a brisk pace, and they realized that they were not in it alone. Unlike the majority of newlyweds who had few visitors, their new home became a revolving door for anyone who sought out the guidance of a kindly priest.

*

In the early months of 1987, the couple learned that they were expecting a baby. They were overjoyed; Nancy was thrilled to deliver the news to her parents that their first grandchild was on the way. For his part, Father George was excited to build his home in harmony with building his Church.

The child, of course, was me. I was born in August of that year.

For the next three years, my mother continued in her job comforted by the proximity of family and friends who played a significant role in helping her care for me.

After three years of relative bliss, living the life they envisioned, my parents felt settled in. They began planning to give me a brother or sister. It was 1990. I had passed my third birthday, and winter was coming (though the temperatures were mild). I was beginning to speak, and starting to build awareness of my surroundings.

In early December, a few days before my mother's 26th birthday, I was struck by a high fever, or at least the symptoms of one.

Given my father's background in medicine, he loved the opportunity to be a caretaker. In spite of his new career choice, he remained passionate about the medical field, always keeping up with the latest advances. He monitored my condition and noticed unusual signs. Out of diligence, he took me to the doctor who suggested that I might have tonsillitis or another infection of sorts.

Upon hearing the diagnosis, something didn't click with my father. After checking with a few other doctors, he took matters into his own hands. Recognizing that my immune levels seemed off track, he performed his own examination at home and assessed that both my spleen and liver appeared to be enlarged.

Without any hesitation, he called a close friend, a well-known pediatrician. He insisted that I be rushed to the hospital. My father understood what this potentially meant, and while he feared the worst, my mother trusted his instinct. Of course, at that moment, she was not aware of what my father feared could be wrong.

Upon arrival at the hospital, the doctors completed my blood work immediately. Shortly thereafter, a conclusion was reached.

At the age of three, I was diagnosed with acute lymphoblastic leukemia (ALL). I was a high-risk case. The outlook was bleak. The doctors projected a grim timeline ahead, and that news catapulted my mother into the heaviest modes of prayer.

Immediately, my father gave the green light to begin treatment. In the coming days, I underwent the trifecta application of steroids, chemo, and radiation. I stayed in the hospital to complete the blood transfusions, went home, and came back for chemo and radiation.

As the days painfully passed into weeks, it became evident that the treatment in Egypt was merely a temporary solution; it was a grasping attempt to buy time. Every time the doctors pulled back on the steroids, I would balloon up and put on significant weight.

My father was faced with a life-altering decision. He recognized that to ensure the outcome for me would be positive, he'd have to relocate my mother, who was now pregnant, away from everything she had ever known.

In spite of fear of the unknown ringing deep in their souls, they knew this was a matter of life or death. There was no other choice. In April of 1991, my parents packed all their possessions and headed to the United States. They had decided upon a hospital called City of Hope in a place called California.

Besides being terrified for the well-being of her son, remember that my mother was also eight months pregnant. She was very close to her parents and envisioned never celebrating another holiday with them. My mother was unsure if she'd ever return home. Moreover, she was scared to deliver a baby without her own mother nearby. How would she manage it all in a strange land?

In stark contrast, my father was in combat mode. He leveraged all his resources; his only focus was my recovery. Just before the move, I was in remission. It was expected that I'd need to undergo another four years of treatment to prevent relapse. For my father that meant finding the best care possible for me, even if it meant traveling halfway around the world with his young family.

Three weeks after we arrived in California, we moved into an apartment in Arcadia. Shortly thereafter, my mother went into labor. I'll never forget that night; my father hustled me out of bed. He called a neighbor and arranged for me to stay with them until I could go to the hospital.

In early June, I met my sister, Trevina. In the coming days, Vina (as she'd come to be known) and I quickly became inseparable. I was pumped to be a brother. I felt like I had a role in the family. I didn't mind at all that I'd no longer be the focal point of my family. In fact, because of my circumstances at the time, I was probably getting too much attention from my parents.

By that point, I had already gone through a lot. But I wasn't dwelling on the past; I was doubling down on the future, and having a baby sister to love and protect was a bright spot for me.

# 3

# All About Me

Both my parents grew up attending Catholic grade schools in Egypt. Granted the public school system was a far cry from the U.S. (which to some doesn't say much), most middle and upper–class families in Egypt were accustomed to paying for private school. Beyond education, religion was essential for a majority of Egyptians and it didn't matter if you were Christian, Muslim, or Jewish. There weren't many atheists. In fact, if someone was a non-believer, they probably kept that to themselves for fear of social retribution.

When we first moved to Long Island, we lived in the town of Syosset which was geographically smack dab in the middle of the island. Historically, the town was recognized for its school district. My parents were encouraged to try it out, and so I was enrolled in kindergarten.

For the first time in my life, I was going to be among an eclectic group of peers who grew up with diverse cultural norms and belief systems. I was going to be different, but so was everyone else. The realization of that was bittersweet. A part of me was ready to see if I could adjust to the broader group, while another was concerned that maybe I would no longer be special.

Two years went by, and things weren't clicking. I struggled to make friends. I still couldn't find common ground with my fellow classmates. I was six years old, so I was aware of my frequent doctor visits. I was the only Egyptian, and perhaps the only natural immigrant in my class as well. My dad was a priest and that definitely was not the norm.

My English was improving but still nothing to write home about. My overall vocabulary was a work-in-progress, and I was fully aware of it. I liked to play and take part in sports during recess, but I was slower than my peers. As you can imagine, most boys that age don't refrain from calling you out or letting you know they've identified your shortcomings.

I struggled to build a foundation for developing my identity, and my parents took note, so they decided to pull me out in second grade. I transferred to Saint Edward the Confessor School, which also happened to be in Syosset.

Upon changing school systems, I was introduced to my first uniform. It was a weird feeling putting on a clip-on tie for the first time; I had no idea what I was getting into. I never had to dress up for school before; the concept was foreign and a little frightening. If they're strict on uniforms than what else are they strict about? Are my parents sending me to some sort of institution?

Just before my first day, I hit a mental reset button. I had learned valuable lessons from the first two years of school; I was very aware that I had to do something different this time around in order to see new results, but I wasn't entirely sure what that would entail.

My mom, however, was more at ease. Whereas she had to do lots of catching up on the material I was previously bringing home, she understood the mission behind a Catholic School education. She felt as if she'd be better prepared to help me. In addition, she was preparing for a change herself. As I was finishing up my last years of treatment, my mom was looking to resume her career.

The administration at Saint Edward's was made aware of my background, and they were familiar with my dad and his role. All things being equal, this seemed like the right move for a multitude of reasons. Outside of my discomfort with the uniform, I was ready to be positive and give it a go.

My first teacher, Mrs. Lane was really friendly; her classroom was warm and welcoming. She changed the themes around the seasons, and had an ability to talk *with* students as opposed to talking at them. She made my transition a little easier. Since, to that point, I had struggled to make many friends, I leaned in on my schoolwork. I earned good grades and stayed out of trouble, but still had no answer to my struggling social life. I blamed it on the other kids; this group had known each other for a couple of years already. Whereas I was coming in late, I was the new kid.

I remember one assignment from that first year in particular: All About Me. We were instructed to dig up old photos, and tell a story of our life on a poster board. Many of my classmates had come in with typical experiences, like that time their family went to a ball game together, or their recent vacation to Disney World. I had no such photos to that point in my life. The story I was going to tell was much different.

I shared pictures of myself as a baby pre-diagnosis, some post-treatment ones as well, but none of them were overly reflective of the battle my body fought (my mother had left those ones out on purpose). Then I shared photos of my family, and immediately got some strange looks.

"How is your dad a priest? Priests don't get married!"

I was seven for crying out loud, and just wanted to fit in. I didn't need yet another obstacle. Of course, given I attended a Catholic school, the majority of the students were Roman Catholic. As far as they were concerned (and most Americans, for that matter) priests didn't marry. I did my best to educate my fellow classmates about cultural differences, about what is 'normal' in Egypt, and the history of the Orthodox Church. But, on Long Island, there was no real awareness of my family's denomination.

Over the next three years, I was continuously tormented for my cultural differences. I tried to rationally articulate these differences, but I was outnumbered. It felt like a battle I was never going to win. The bullying would start as early as the morning bus ride, and it felt like there was no end in sight.

My mother had been working at that point, so she was not able to participate in PTA meetings, or when I was in the Cub Scouts. A lot of times, I found myself coming home expressing grief around my differences, and it was hard for her to grasp the picture I painted. Even though she'd had a long day at the office, I remember her doing her best to guide me and teach me.

Both her and my dad encouraged me to partake in all sorts of activities to develop my interests. I had trial periods with music where I took on the drums, then the trumpet, and then the clarinet. Ultimately, I concluded that music wasn't for me; I had no rhythm and I wasn't interested enough. I tried baseball, but that seemed like a lost cause from day one. The only sport that I stuck with was basketball. Once I found something that worked, my parents pushed me to stick with it. Basketball became an outlet for me in the face of hardship from other areas of my life.

Typically, my father took care of the household tasks, preparing meals for my sister and me. I recall him waking up early in the morning and helping my sister with her hair as my mom got ready for work. He was not a pro by any means, but he knew what had to be done and tried his best.

*

My elementary school years tried me deeply; they wore me down. I continued to do well academically, and that was a bright spot. I didn't give up on basketball, even though my speed was an issue whenever I was on the court. I spent late nights shooting hoops alone. I knew that I was going to have to work twice as hard as everybody else to attain the results that I was seeking.

At home, my bedroom was covered wall–to–wall in Michael Jordan posters. I collected his trading cards; I watched every game I could; I read every article I got a hold of; I memorized his stat lines. I was obsessed. I was taken by Jordan's greatness; he embodied hard work and dedication to his craft. You could see in his eyes the obsession with winning on every play.

I bought into his message. I believed that I could accomplish about anything I set my mind to. To be honest, I had a chip on my shoulder, and because of Michael, I envisioned myself proving everyone wrong. I believed that the endless days and nights playing in my backyard, rain or shine, until I made ten free throws in a row would pay off. I believed that one day I'd get my shot to compete on a level playing field with everyone else.

By this time, I was in third grade. Saint Edward's ran a popular Catholic Youth Organization (CYO) program in the area; I signed up as soon as became I eligible. I looked forward to every single practice and game. I wanted to play, but I also wanted to learn how to be a good teammate. I strove to be the best player that I could be.

In my mind, this was a stealth 'friendship' program as well. A way for me to force my teammates to be my friends, even if it was only once a week. For those two hours, I had friends, and that felt good. I even cajoled my dad to play with me when I was getting started. It never crossed my mind that he had no prior experience with a basketball, he was more of a soccer player in his youth.

Physically, I knew my weaknesses. I couldn't drive left; I favored my right, leaving me exposed to defenders. But this wasn't the pros, it was an intramural CYO program—most kids there were not skilled. Additionally, however, I was not very strong. Despite being very active, I never built up much muscle during my years of treatment. I was not fast, and that haunted me. For the life of me, as a child between the ages of eight and eleven, I could not make sense of why I was always last to finish on those suicide lines.

I was pushing myself to the max, pouring my heart and soul into every play. But, no matter what I did and no matter how bad I wanted it, I could not increase my speed. It destroyed my psyche. I accepted that I was slow, and I began to accept that it was a part of my constitution. It killed me to see other guys running with such ease, but I was out of solutions.

I compensated for it by working on my jump shot. I studied proper form—watching tutorials and asking coaches for advice. I attended an after-school program that was run by Mr. Swift, our Phys Ed instructor. I spent every afternoon working on my shot in the gym. I was beginning to build a competitive edge. I believed I could make a shot from anywhere on the court. It was the first time I uncovered any form of athletic ability.

Around fifth grade I began to find my groove. I was confident when I'd get called into a game, and I wasn't scared to shoot if I was open. As a ten-year-old, I was a seasoned intramural CYO player; I understood the pace of games and the intensity level. The thing about an intramural league is that there are no try-outs; so long as you pay the admission fee, you're on a team.

It was around this time when I noticed that the more substantial competition was shifting to the 'travel' team. Those guys had shiny jerseys with their last names engraved; they'd talk up the intensity of their games as if they were going to be on SportsCenter the next day. I felt like I was settling where I was. I wanted to figure out a way to get one of those jerseys.

Of course, making the travel team meant I had to try out, and two years in a row I didn't make the cut. The coaches weren't shy about the reason: my speed was the factor. Finally, the third year, I made the 'B-Team.' I was thrilled, even though it was exactly what it sounds like; it was the team no one paid any attention to. That didn't bother me; I wanted that jersey. I wanted any chance to prove myself. I was re-energized and zoned in for success.

The season started, and it was evident early on that our team was not stacked up sufficiently against the competition. Early on, the coach used me sparingly, but—as the season progressed and our record got worse—I saw my limited playing time regress to nothing. Our coach had two sons who both played on the team. While they were both athletic and skilled, they had proven to be difficult teammates. They threw fits during practice and argued during games. Considering the fact they were both starters, they were not exemplary when it came to leadership.

My parents attended games when their schedules permitted. Even though my dad was usually tied up on weekends, he did his best to attend when possible. Given the state of our team, he was thrown off by the fact that I was rarely given a shot to be on the court. But it was not his way to be confrontational with the coach or question the man's judgement.

One winter night, after another loss, I was finally at my wit's end. I approached my coach and asked how was it possible that I wasn't being utilized. Without hesitation, he pointed to my speed. My heart sunk. That night at home, I slammed shut the door to my bedroom. My face went straight into my pillow, and soon it was soaked in tears.

My mother felt helpless; she hated to see me so distraught, and couldn't find the right words to make me feel better. My dad understood the situation. I heard him picking up the phone. All of a sudden, my cries were muted by the booming voice coming from the other room.

My father laid into my coach. For the very first time I heard the words, "You have no idea what this child has been through." Dad proceeded to walk my coach through all of the treatment I had undertaken. How, in spite of all that, I keep fighting in order to have my moment.

I didn't understand why I was slow, but hearing my father talk about the effects of chemo got me thinking: perhaps I'd never be able to keep up with the other kids. I did not fully comprehend what chemo was, or how it could slow me down, but I vowed to not let it beat me.

It was the first time I had seen my dad put someone in their place over my physical ability. And, frankly, it was scary hearing him scold another grown man. Yet it was reassuring at the same time. My father had my back. That felt good because, when it came to proving myself on the basketball court, I had considered it a lonely and personal battle—much like my battle with leukemia.

Needless to say, the next basketball game that came around, I was back on the court.

# 4

# Not Enough Room in the ICU

When I was in third grade, my parents moved us from Syosset to a new home in the town of Huntington. Fortunately, it wasn't much of a disruption; I didn't need to change my school. Simultaneously, I was getting a bigger room and more space outside to ride my bike and play ball. So, all things considered, a win–win.

Shortly after we moved in, I completed my treatment and, with regards to my health, was given the green light. Life was normal. My parents treated me like all the other parents did their children; I didn't receive any special attention. For them, too, it was a breath of fresh air; their nightmare was officially over.

I still struggled to find my place socially, but I wasn't giving up. If anything, I felt reborn knowing that I'd have fewer doctor appointments on my calendar.

A few years in the new neighborhood went by, and I was enduring seventh grade. I had hit a wall trying to fit in at Saint Edward's, so I pushed my parents to transfer me to the local public school. I wanted a fresh start.

I had been classmates with the same thirty or so students for five years at that point. There was nothing that I could say or do that would all of a sudden make them accept me. In fact, even the good days seemed transient. I needed desperately to change up my routine before high school started in a year or so.

My parents agreed. And, boom, there I was—at the local middle school—in a brand new environment again. The school year was about halfway complete at that point, so my focus was on getting acclimated academically (my go-to safe spot). The assignments and workload at the new school were more rigorous, and as someone who was always a top performer, I was forced to push myself harder than I had been used to. The months rushed by.

June approached and everyone, myself included, was getting ready for summer vacation. Right about then I started noticing some unusual symptoms: horrible headaches that pounded for long bouts, nausea even if I had not been overeating. My body felt out of sync. I mentioned these symptoms to my dad, and he didn't display an alarming level of concern. However, he would casually check in every day or two to see if anything had changed.

In the back of his mind, my father feared the worst. His medical background had taught him about the long-term side effects of radiation exposure, and I was approaching the ten-year mark of my diagnosis. In spite of his suspicions, he didn't jump to a conclusion. Rather, he calmly set up an appointment with my pediatrician.

A few days of discomfort passed as my symptoms persisted. At the doctor's office, the doctor suggested there was a virus going around. He felt that, most likely, I had fallen victim. My father was not comforted at all with the diagnosis, but he listened politely then we returned home.

It was mid-summer by this point. I'd been attending a church camp. Since I was not contagious, my parents let me carry on with my life. One day there was a field trip planned to a rock climbing gym. I quickly scaled the first two or three levels with ease. Then, all of a sudden, the pounding in my head rung louder than ever before. I quickly descended and rushed to a restroom to vomit. I couldn't make any sense of it; something was off. I felt as though my body was failing me, and I was only twelve. I had no idea what was wrong, but I knew I needed help.

That afternoon my dad picked me up, and I told him what happened. He immediately sprung into action. He scheduled new doctor appointments for more opinions and, upon our next visit, he refused to accept the same diagnosis. In fact, he insisted that I be referred for a CT scan. Once the doctor agreed, I was quickly taken to the hospital. When the scan was completed, and the results came in, I was informed that I should get comfortable. I would be staying there for a while.

For the first time in several years, I was asked to clench my fist and get ready—an IV was coming my way. Oddly, it was a moment of reminiscence. I didn't miss the needles and the blood, but I'd been a patient for such a significant portion of my life. I though that maybe this is a part of who I am.

Unbeknownst to me, the doctors found a mass in the right frontal lobe of my brain; it was about the size of a golf ball. They proceeded to give me an MRI after the original CT scan. That would give them more clarity on what they were dealing with. The concern, of course, was whether or not the mass was cancerous. But, given my history, it seemed unlikely that it could be anything besides cancer.

It was the last week of July when I was admitted to the hospital. By early August, I was approaching my thirteenth birthday. That's when I was notified that we were going to transfer hospitals. From the moment I was admitted, I was given very few details around the actual prognosis. Instead, I was given plenty of reassurance that everything was going to be okay; I had nothing to worry about. Everyone who visited me in the hospital, from my parents and relatives to friends from school, kept my spirits up. I was catered to from every angle. I had very little to complain about given the gravity of the situation (of which I was unaware).

Vina was at my side the entire time. You could feel the empathy in her heart from a mile away. She was like my personal usher, taking people in and out of the hospital room. Among those guests was Emo and George, childhood friends who were at my bedside for several days leading up to the surgery.

The thought of cancer never crossed my mind. The idea that I would not resume a healthy life a few short days later also seemed outrageous. As far as I was concerned, there was a procedure of some sort or another coming my way; the doctor was going to do what doctors do. Since I was going to be under anesthesia, I won't feel it. Then everything would be fine.

My dad knew me perhaps better than I knew myself. He knew that if I found out how dire the circumstances were, I'd likely deteriorate emotionally. The last thing a child needs before heading into an intense brain surgery is emotional distress. It was August 8, 2000: my thirteenth birthday. I was taken into an operating room at NYU Medical Center. The anesthesiologist asked me a question or two and, before I knew it, I was out cold. The surgery to remove a potential tumor was underway.

\*

Six hours later, I was awoken by the surgeon. My eyes blinked, struggling to see the light. I had no idea what hit me. As a child, I discovered my high threshold for pain when I encountered my first spinal tap. This was different; this was probably as close as one gets to full-on paralysis. I felt paralyzed by the casting all over my body. It hurt to think; it hurt to blink. I was in a physical state that I had never experienced before.

I was on all types of medication: morphine, in particular, was unique. I recall hallucinating, imagining that I was on the TV game show, *The Price is Right*. I thought that my dad was Bob Barker (absolutely no resemblance). I felt a level of pain that I don't wish upon anyone. Even the slightest noise in the room could stir up painful vibrations throughout my body. I couldn't move a single bone in my body.

The child next to me in the Pediatric ICU was having a seizure. It was terrifying to witness. His parents were in a state of panic, screaming at the nurses for help. I was trapped in bed, motionless and useless, unable to help anyone around me or even myself.

I struggled to put this child's bout in perspective. I thought darkly, "There's not enough room in this ICU for both of us. One of us will have to go." It was that moment post-surgery when I hit rock bottom. Never in my life did I feel so physically helpless. The realization that things couldn't get worse was the only thing that allowed me to push forward.

We were awaiting the results of the surgery to come out; the level of suspense was at an all-time high. My parents deserved a miracle for all of their prayers, their faith, and their sacrifice. Fortunately, that is what they got; the mass was benign. My head was stapled back together with what proved to be a life-altering scar. Unlike injection tube scars, which can be hidden underneath garments, this one was glaring; it was ugly. Haircuts have never been the same since.

"So when can I play basketball?"

That was my first question to the surgeon. I'll never forget the stern look in my mother's eye. She knew that I'd be taking it easy for the foreseeable future. To her dismay, within weeks, I was out on our driveway 'basketball court' with staples still in my head. I refused to be slowed down after encountering my breaking point in that recovery room.

You see, the interesting thing is that although those couple of weeks signified the end of another horrible episode for my parents, it marked the beginning of the rest of my life. I was coming into myself with a vengeance I never felt before.

My life felt like a ball game to me. During the first half, the world was scoring against me in every way possible. Up until then, the message had been that I wouldn't make it. I wasn't healthy enough; I wasn't fast enough; I wasn't cool enough. I was different, and nobody likes different. But, after I left that hospital, I mapped out how I would attack the rest of my life. I understood the path ahead of me would involve detours, but the destination started to become clear.

Never again was I to doubt my ability to overcome adversity; never again was I to allow myself to be defeated by what people say. It was time to show myself that barriers are meant to be broken. Even with the cards stacked against me, I was going to come out victorious.

*

By the time I got back home from the hospital, summer was winding down, and eighth grade was right around the corner. I wasn't settled in at my school, given that I just transferred there a few months before. I was overweight from all the medication and from being confined to a hospital bed eating anything I could get my hands on. I was a sucker for Taco Bell, and I had my guests pick up orders for me before they came to visit.

Also, I was extremely self-conscious around my scar; it took up the whole right side of my head. Regardless of what direction my hair was combed, you couldn't miss it. I hated the way I looked in the mirror. My parents had exhausted their emotional capacity over the summer. I could tell they felt like they dodged a bullet, so I let them breathe a little when it came to helping me fight my battles.

Soon Labor Day came around, and I was back roaming the halls trying to figure out how to work the new locker and navigate my schedule. In Spanish class, the teacher asked us to go around the room and introduce ourselves. We needed select a native Spanish name to use throughout the year from a list she provided. Before I could even get to name I picked, I heard chuckles from the back.

"What's a Bishoy?" Just what I needed to kick off the year.

I didn't know the kid personally; however, he was your typical jock. The guys liked him and laughed at his antics; the girls flocked to him. I kept composed for that moment in the classroom, but I was raging on the inside. As soon as class was over, I confronted him in the hall. I gave the jerk a shove and had a colorful word or two for him. Mind you, this was David vs. Goliath on all fronts. He was stronger than me. Then, before I knew it, we were separated; I found myself in the administrator's office.

I was scared; I had never gotten in any sort of trouble before. Unlike at Saint Edward's, where at least the teachers knew me well enough to understand I was not an instigator, I was in a new school with a new administration. I was up against a beloved student; his word against mine.

"Am I going to get suspended?" I thought. "How pissed are my parents going to be? Will justice be served? Will anyone hear me out? I'm a good kid. Why can't people just accept me? Why can't I figure this out?"

Fortunately, neither of us landed any punches; no one was actually hurt. The administrator decided to set up a peer mediation session. It was the first time I had ever heard of such a thing, but I was relieved to avoid suspension. High school was on the horizon. I was going to apply to Saint Anthony's High School, and didn't want any negative glitches on my record.

However, I didn't really know what peer mediation entailed. I guess it sounded self-explanatory. I was looking forward to drawing out a solution and putting the matter behind me. I wanted to look ahead and continue navigating the school/social life balance.

The whole scuffle was a momentary lapse in judgment for me. I was so focused on making the most of my opportunity at a new school that, once my plan was disrupted, I was rattled. I'm not a fighter by any means, but I saw no other option. That kid had to know I wasn't going to tolerate another year of abuse.

The jock and I entered the room for our session. It was a small office with somewhat dim lighting. The two of us sat down with the administrator. This man also happened to be one of the football coaches, so he knew the other student.

The session protocol was reasonably straightforward; we both voiced our version of events, then talked about how we would address things moving forward. I was nervous, my voice quivered as I spoke. Meanwhile I picked up on the fact that the jock was calm, almost arrogantly so, like this was a waste of his time. He didn't seem phased at all. He understood that we were going to go through the motions of reconciling; it was theater. Then, after we walked out, we'd carry on with our lives.

In fact, he was spot on. Once we left that room, it was as if nothing ever happened. I realized a few things. Firstly, I had to release some of my edges; I shouldn't have been at such a tipping point. Secondly, it clicked with me that this whole 'fitting in' thing was going to be a process; it would involve rejection at times. It was one of the first times that I learned the importance of embracing failure as a launching pad for getting back up and trying again, perhaps doing something different to draw different results. Lastly, I dared myself to make that kid like me.

I knew it would involve lots of trial and error, but I figured if I could get Goliath to like David then maybe I'd pick up on a trick or two that I could apply to other relationships. As the years went by, the two of us found ourselves in the same circle. We hung out together frequently, and our scuffle never once came up. I persisted in learning out how to be his friend; it was an accomplishment that rung heavily with me as I navigated those years.

# Homeroom on September 11th

Ever since fourth grade, I had my heart set on Saint Anthony's High School. Even though I switched school systems, I was persistent that, come time for high school, it would be the school for me. The combination of its highly touted academics and its reputation as a powerhouse that produced some of the most recognized athletes on Long Island. I didn't even play football, but I was drawn to that *Friday Night Lights* aura. Saint Anthony's had that; it was always featured on the pages of Newsday, our local newspaper.

I had to take an entrance exam and go through an application process. Luckily, I got accepted. It was back to wearing a uniform, and this time around I was more comfortable with a tie, upgrading from clip-ons to the real-thing. I had returned to my average weight; I no longer showed signs of surgery or my treatment. I was an ordinary awkward-looking fourteen-year-old, yet I exuded more confidence than I had ever before. Maybe it was blind, but it was confidence nonetheless.

Kids came from all over the island, from different schools and all kinds of backgrounds. There were familiar faces in the crowd, students from Saint Edward's and my good old pal from peer mediation. I wasn't bothered by them, since most of us were in a similar boat, looking to get settled in and make friends.

The first day of school, all the freshman students were brought into the auditorium. Like many Catholic schools, we started with Mass and a welcome message from the administration. Then we were escorted to our homerooms, which were set up alphabetically. These configurations were intended to last throughout the entire four years of high school, so it was understood that you'd want to get comfortable with this particular set of classmates.

Kicking off freshman year was daunting; the hallways looked immense, and the older students appeared a lot older than they actually were. It was clear we were fish out of water. The first week was hectic. We were getting adjusted and each teacher made a point to emphasize we were now in the 'big leagues.' The expectation was that we'd be more independent; the notion of accountability was taking on a new meaning.

As the first weekend came around, I remember coming home with positive reports for my parents. I told them that my first week went well; I was excited about all the opportunity that the school presented. There was a team for any sport you could think of; there were clubs for whatever your hobby was. With that many students, I was bound to find a group of friends at some point; the odds were in my favor. My parents were relieved to see that I was adapting. They encouraged me to keep exploring everything that the school had to offer.

Monday came around, just a typical day. I attended an after-school event, got home around seven, had a late dinner, and finished my homework. When I awoke on Tuesday morning, I was a little tired, but it was too early in the year to play the 'sick' card. I knew that I couldn't miss the school bus, because my dad had to get to an appointment in Manhattan that day.

I rolled out of bed and dragged myself to school. I was still figuring out my schedule and the locations of my classes, but before I knew it, I was in homeroom. Usually, during homeroom, there was a short prayer and announcements over the loudspeaker. This time, something was off. Teachers were asking students if they had parents that worked in Manhattan. Anyone who raised their hand was spoken to privately. I was a little curious as to what was going on. My mother had worked in the city for several years in a location downtown near the World Trade Center. However, just the year before, she had moved to a new job in Long Island.

The principal came on over the loudspeaker; he announced that there had been a dire headline in the news that day. Although the report was still being gathered, it was critical that any students with parents that work in Manhattan identify themselves; they would be allowed to call their loved ones.

He shared with us that planes crashed into the World Trade Center that morning, and the towers had collapsed. He mentioned that several people had died as a result, but it was also too soon to share an estimate. Without visuals, it was tough to wrap my head around the announcement and precisely how bad this really was. I went home that day knowing something terrible had happened, lots of questions circling my head.

*

I walked into the house and found my dad glued to the TV. He told me that he never made it into the boroughs because. as he was listening to radio, they instructed everyone to avoid bridges and tunnels at all costs. He was tuned into all of the reports, trying to make sense of the images on TV. My mother shook her head, thinking that could have been her just a year prior.

At that point, there was a universal acceptance that this was a terrorist attack. As far as I was concerned at fourteen years old growing up in America, the idea that any group would purposely attack innocent people in a fashion so horrific was unthinkable. Even my parents, who I grant had experienced more of global politics than myself, were momentarily taken aback. They had seen hate like this in Egypt since Copts (as members of the Coptic Orthodox Church are known) have a history of facing persecution at the hands of terrorist organizations. Although my parents deeply missed their home country, they believed that something like this could, in no way, follow them to America. Tragically, they were wrong. In his capacity as a spiritual leader, my father spent the next several weeks helping many people cope and understand the events of, what came to be called, 9/11.

Uncertainty abounded over the next few days. Every day, I'd come home and ask my dad for updates. I grew incredibly proud of being an American during that period. I remember chills down my back as I watched President Bush threw the first pitch at the Yankee game after the attacks. There was a unified sense of strength shared amongst New Yorkers. I felt it sitting on the couch in our living room. My father hates baseball, yet he was watching right behind me, fully engaged with the patriotism at Yankee Stadium.

The pieces were coming together about the attackers and their origins. I was getting a crash course on Middle East history. It was all new to me. Up to that point, I wasn't into politics. And, when it came to history, if it wasn't on the exam, I wasn't paying attention. Regardless of faith, I couldn't understand how any group of people could one: be this angry to want to do this; and two, pull off a plan like this given all of the things that should have gone wrong. It took me a long time to wrap my head around all of it.

One of the significant political headlines in those weeks was that of "increased racial profiling" around the United States. The Sikh community, in particular, had fallen victim to misguided attacks. I thought to myself as I saw these reports, this could be troublesome for a variety of communities who don't share in a hateful ideology. I looked at my father in our kitchen: he had a beard; he was Middle

Eastern. But he also had a glaring silver crucifix wrapped around his neck. I thought to myself, "People can't be that foolish."

The 9/11 attacks were a topic of conversation for a long time. Saint Anthony's provided the resources at their disposal to help students cope with the aftermath. We were looking for answers, and there was no clear timeline around when things would feel normal again. I was still trying to figure out how to expand my base of friends. I did feel wariness from some folks who didn't know my background, but I refused to let it get to me.

Typically, in the cafeteria, I found myself shifting tables a fair amount, trying to find a group that I'd click with. I liked to use the opportunity to meet new people. One day, a few weeks after the attack, I found myself amongst a group of guys. They were loud, a bunch of jokesters, and I wanted to get in on the fun.

One of them (his name was Alex) turned to me, and asked, "What's your story?" I gave him a dumbfounded look. My instincts were sharp, and I didn't need any trouble.

"You look like one of those Muslim guys," he taunted. I told him to cut it out. I tried to make it clear that I wasn't looking for a fight. He kept egging me on, but I wasn't taking the bait. Then he upped his verbal assault.

"Hey, man," he said, "I saw your dad pick you up. He looks like he could double as Bin Laden." My mind froze.

For an eternal moment, emotions of anger rose to the surface. The darkest musings of isolation flashed in my head. I was not going to allow Alex, or anyone like him, to dictate my place in the social arena. I needed to act; I wasn't going to be an outcast again.

His words took me over the edge. I jumped over one of his friends to the other side of the table and threw a punch. It was my very first punch, but it was bittersweet. The kid was a punk, and he deserved it, but I found myself alone again with no one to turn to. And, this time, it was in front of a packed high school cafeteria.

I went on the defensive over a remark that was utterly baseless, but, given the times, that was reality. I had to set the record straight.

I took solace in the fact that the Saint Anthony's administration was on my side. Even if the students did not understand, the people who ran the show at the school (mostly Franciscan brothers clearly aware of my father and his position) did. Thankfully, they did not tolerate it.

# House Party

Freshman year flew by; I was focused on making as many friends as possible. I didn't care for cliques or for fitting in with one group over another. I wanted to put my adaptability on display. I had grown up watching my dad engage with people from all walks of life. Given how admired he was, I wanted to emulate his skillset to the best of my ability. The problem was that, as the end of the school year approached, I found myself with acquaintances but no real friends. On the bright side, I had no enemies, and I was no longer being bullied.

Looking back, at the age of fourteen, my personality didn't have much of an edge. I wasn't shy, but I wasn't much of a risk taker; I preferred to stay out of trouble. I had a sense of pride in my track record of never being in a situation where I deserved disciplinary action, whether it was from my parents or from the administration at school. In the two instances where I got in trouble—riding the line on my generous self-assessment—I felt that I was the victim.

Additionally, I wasn't good at figuring out where I best fit in. And, since everyone wore a uniform, there wasn't much room for self-expression. To figure out who I could mesh with, I'd have to dig below the surface to truly understand my classmates.

The film *American Pie* had been released two years prior, and the sequel was on its way. For me, the series was iconic in giving mainstream audiences a portrayal of the high school party scene. I wasn't clueless, I knew you wanted to be in on the scene. You wanted to be one of the insiders who had all the information. As I got invited to parties, like many high school kids, I became crafty around what I told my parents. I trusted myself to stay out of trouble, but the less my folks knew the better.

My body had always been sensitive to foreign substances. Even a substantial meal could make me feel unwell at times, so I was wary of what I ingested. As a result, I had no interest in drugs. Smoking a joint never appealed to me. I wasn't judgmental of others; to each their own. I just knew there was a chance my body would react poorly. That being said, I still wanted to have fun, so I leaned on alcohol. Bud Light was the beer of choice for us Long Island kids.

On the party front, every week someone new was hosting, and every week it would be the talk of the school. If you threw a party, you were instantly well regarded. It was like you were the hero of the weekend and the five days that followed. Over my sophomore year, the scene started to pick up, and I became more integrated within it. However, the issue was we were running out of houses. The kids were desperate; they needed somewhere to go. It was the perfect opportunity for someone new to step in.

I toyed with the idea. This would definitely help me in the social arena. But I also had to weigh the risk-to-reward factor. Parties had a way of getting out of hand. I needed to feel things out first. At home one night, I told my parents that I'd be having some friends over. They were receptive. My mom was happy I'd be bringing some of my friends over, since she hadn't met too many of my classmates. The one little detail I left out was the number of people that were coming over. But, honestly, I had no gauge on that. It was literally my first rodeo. Who knew if kids would even show up? Moreover, we lived in your average size home. Not small quarters by any means, but not a mansion either. This would definitely not be one of those situations where you partied in the basement while the rest of the house is oblivious to the noise.

"It's time to put it out there and roll the dice," I thought.

I settled on date, got my folks to agree to it, and started telling people. Word travels quickly down the halls of a high school. Soon classmates were coming by my locker to say they were excited. Momentum was building up; this was really going to happen. I was living in the moment, thrilled by all of the attention I was getting. But I wasn't keeping count of how many people were saying 'yes.' Anytime I started to feel overwhelmed by the response, I'd suppress those feelings and convince myself that everything was going to be fine. There would be enough space in the house, enough red Solo cups, and enough alcohol. Most importantly, I convinced myself that my parents won't suspect anything.

\*

Friday night came around. My party was the talk of the school. It wasn't just a few classmates anymore; it wasn't a particular clique or two. Word had gotten to the neighboring high school as well. I was getting nervous, I suppressed the anxiety.

"Once this is all over," I thought, "People will have a reason to remember my name."

After school, on the night of the event, I feverishly cleaned up the basement, taking care to remove any fragile items. I set up the ice, the music, and bowls of pretzels and chips. Before I knew it, it was 7:30 and the first couple of guests were arriving. They came in to politely say "hello" to my parents who were in the kitchen, then made their way downstairs to the basement. In a subtle (yet not so subtle) fashion, as each guest descended the stairs, beers were pulled out of jacket pockets. The night was underway.

Over the next hour, small groups trickled in. To my mind, everything was under control. I went back and forth between the kitchen and the basement, managing my parents and the guests. Around 9:30, I took a moment to look outside. Our house sat on a tranquil tree-lined street. But that night, the street was lit with cars. I saw a huge group of about twenty people making their way over; one of them had a hockey bag.

"This should be interesting," I thought.

My poor parents could not keep track of who was who anymore. I smiled to them sheepishly as I followed the group of twenty down into the basement. Suddenly, I realized there wasn't a foot of space; we were 'at capacity.' I ran back upstairs. More people were still walking in. I had to do something, so I directed them to the garage. I was starting to feel that maybe I was in over my head.

My mother did her best to be patient, but after seeing me rush around for cleaning supplies to mop up several spills, she was done. It time to investigate. With purpose, she walked down the stairs. To her dismay, it was a scene straight out of *American Pie*. My mother shut off the light, turned off the music, and at the top of her lungs instructed everybody to call their parents.

Realizing the party was over, most of my classmates scurried upstairs to call their parents. In those short few hours, some had outdone themselves with drinking. They weren't moving so quickly. Those and few others weren't ready for the party to end. But they dutifully complied and exited the basement.

To be honest, I wasn't ashamed. Actually, I felt a sense of relief because, with each spilled beer from a red Solo cup, the basement had been descending into chaos. I knew I was going to get a stern talking to. But I figured, at worst, I'd be responsible for cleaning up. This wasn't worth grounding me for, right?

As I headed upstairs to say "goodbye" to the kids who were leaving, all of a sudden a classmate came running in, looking disheveled. He had run as fast he could from down the block.

"What happened?" I asked.

"Don't mind me," he said between quick gasps, "We need to call an ambulance!" My heart sank.

The two of us hustled outside, and rushed back down the street. One of our classmates, the guy who brought the hockey bag earlier, had clearly overindulged and needed help. It turns out the hockey bag was stuffed with bottles of vodka. We helped the guy to his feet, and brought him back to the house.

Right then and there, my mom's instructions to the kids changed from "Please call your parents" to "Everybody out." My dad, meanwhile, had remained calm. To him, this was nothing new. He took the student who was sick and sat him up. My father took care of him until help arrived. Ultimately, the boy was rushed to the hospital; he had his stomach pumped. Fortunately, he was back in school a few days after.

My mother was mortified at what she had seen. She couldn't assemble the words to express the horror I put her through that night. She prayed for the well–being of the student with the hockey bag. That was her primary concern. Then, in the days that followed, after it was clear he'd recovered, I felt the wrath of my mother's disappointment. My dad felt the same as her, and that stung.

When I went back to school the next week, kids were patting me on the back. They had a ton of fun and were asking me when the next time would be. Even though the party ended on short notice, for the majority of my classmates, it was a thrill.

No doubt it came at a substantial expense, but their happiness made me feel like it was worth it. I gave them something they wanted and, as a result, they drew closer to me. It was up to me to capitalize on the moment. To this day, I smile when somebody says "Remember that party at Bro-shoy's."

# Enthusiasm in the Face of Failure

# From the Grill to the Call Center

Persistence has always been second nature for me. As a child I was pretty whiny; I nagged a lot if I was told I couldn't have something. I was the kid that wouldn't shut up, and I had it down to a science. In the back of my mind, I knew that my health issues gave me the upper hand. My tactics worked because others felt bad for me. However, as I grew, nagging eventually lost its impact. Over time, I pivoted to another means of getting my way: persuasion. To be successful in the art of persuasion, one must prepare for rejection. Persuasion involves having answers for potential hesitations, and those answers need to be delivered with clarity and confidence.

During high school, my biggest sell was myself. I persuaded others that they wanted to become my friend (when it actually was the other way around). This is the period where I learned how to be a salesman. The key to being a good at sales is to make the buyer feel as if they are purchasing on their own accord. You don't want them to ever perceive that they are being sold. And I knew the type of people I wanted to surround myself with. My attraction was the go-getters: kids that challenged themselves, the ones that filled a room with positive energy. I think that, focusing on those qualities in others helped to nurture them in myself as well.

Junior year was busy. I was gearing up for the SATs. The word 'college' came up at least once a week in conversation. And, I was on the verge of driving a car, with all of the freedom and changes that would bring. In New York, the legal driving age (for a learner's permit) is sixteen. As students prepared for the new privilege to come, parents calculated the costs for gas, car insurance, and other incidentals that were associated with a teenage driver.

The majority of students picked up jobs that year to earn some cash in anticipation of getting behind the wheel. My parents were more concerned with my education. They knew that it was an intensive year, one that had significance for my future education. They were hesitant when I said I wanted to apply for a job. I didn't really need the money; my parents were happy to help me out financially. However my 'fear of missing out' was kicking in. I saw my friends working a variety of jobs, and I was antsy to test out the market for myself.

Though I was on a job hunt, I didn't have the slightest idea how to approach it. At sixteen, I didn't feel qualified for much. I had no experience, and only a handful of employers would even consider someone so young.

"The one place I always see kids my age," I thought, "is working the cash registers at fast food counters."

So I walked into the local McDonald's and asked for a job application. A few days later I got a call from the store manager. After a brief interview sitting inside the dining area, he offered me my first job (at a minimum wage, of course).

"That was easy enough," I thought.

I was excited to get started. I envisioned myself being a star behind the cash register, the first face that customers would see, bringing smiles to customers' faces—going the extra mile for anyone who walked into the restaurant. And, since I was a good math student, I even looked forward to the great responsibility of managing the money.

On my first day at McDonald's, I was eager to get started. I put on my uniform and name tag with pride, and greeted my manager, awaiting his instructions. I assumed I was going to receive a crash course on using the cash register. Instead, he introduced to Dave, the assistant manager. Dave took me to the back where they stored the ingredients and made sandwiches to order.

"Hmm, okay" I thought, "Maybe this is where everyone starts off before being able to work in the front."

Dave had me going in and out of the freezer throughout the day, picking up different kinds of meat and chicken. The packages were heavy, and it was cold in those freezers, especially since my uniform was a short–sleeved polo.

"I won't complain yet," I thought, "this is part of the process."

After a couple days, Dave showed me how to work the grill. I'm not sure what the labor laws were back then, but it felt odd to be given that responsibility considering I was the youngest employee. I assumed anything would be better stomping back into the tundra of the freezer. I was wrong. Every night that I came home from working the grill I smelled like a Big Mac. I was losing my patience; this was not the job that I thought I had applied for.

Nearly three weeks in, even that I worked a number of hours, the paychecks felt pretty slim. It didn't seem like there were plans to take me off the grill anytime soon , so I asked Dave when I'd be able to work the front. He told me to set up a meeting with the manager, so I did.

That day, I was behind a hot grill again. I was sweating through my shirt, and my pores wreaked of the stench from the cooking oil. As I flipped the burgers, there was a big splash of oil! I screamed. Then I looked down at my arm to see a glaring burn, it was nasty. That was the tipping point. I was done. It's one thing to do an honest day's work of manual labor, but it's another to go home with a scar on your arm for a measly $7 per hour.

I spoke to the manager later that night. I told him that I had interviewed for a job on the register; it was my expectation that I would be assigned there soon. He said that was not his plan; instead he wanted to keep me in the back. I quit right then and there.

At a young age, I learned the importance of not letting someone else dictate your value because, if you do, the chances are that they will undervalue you. Fortunately, I didn't need this job to make a living. My parents, as I said, were happy to help me out, and actually preferred that I stay focused on my studies.

I realize that I had the luxury, if you will, of being able to choose my future at the moment. I had the freedom to walk out of a bad circumstance. I also learned that I was not the type of person who thrived in that kind of environment, I'd rather keep my hands clean during the work day.

*

In the coming weeks, I decided to give the whole job thing another go around; I knew there had to be a better way.

"Kids my age are looking in the same places for the same kind of job," I thought. "Perhaps I should step outside the box a bit and try something different."

I pulled up the Pennysaver, a local magazine that had a Help Wanted section. It seemed that most of the ads were for odd jobs that I had no interest in. However, when the next week rolled around, at the very top of the section it read, "Investment Firm seeking Telemarketers $12/hour+Commission." That was double the rate I got paid at. I was intrigued, and showed the ad to my dad. He gave his approval, so I sent an email to state my interest.

I was invited to the firm for an interview; the parking lot was lined up with an array of luxury vehicles. As I walked into the lobby, I saw it was filled with people hustling from one meeting to another. They all looked sharp and professional in their expensive suits with dazzling watches on their wrists. I was mesmerized.

"Did I just hit the jackpot?" I thought.

Soon I was escorted into the office of the hiring manager, Kyle. The two of us hit it off immediately. He was a smooth talker; he had swag, but he also was incredibly kind. He explained to me what my function would be: his team was responsible for hosting local seminars pitching investment solutions; my role would be to call on folks all over Long Island and invite them to attend.

I got home that day ecstatic. I told my dad that I wanted to be like Kyle one day. I wanted to dress like that, and have the ability to talk like that. I wanted to be able to sell anyone.

I was the youngest employee again, but this time it played to my favor. I had no reason to be cynical like some of the salespeople. This was my first time at bat, so to speak; I pounded away at those phones. I dialed twenty-five homes per hour, and never let a "not interested" response deter me. I believed that every rejection got me closer to my next sale.

After a couple of weeks, I felt comfortable; I had my routine down pat. The workdays would fly by. Kyle was happy with the results I produced and, more importantly, he was tremendously encouraging of my positive attitude. He taught me the importance of presentation. There's a fine line between looking polished and approachable versus arrogant. Kyle represented everything I wanted out of a career. Even if I couldn't explain the products that he was selling, I knew I wanted to one day be able to sell them.

In spite of telemarketing not being the sexiest job (I didn't get the same attention as my friends who were lifeguards), I absolutely loved the work. In fact, I was making more than most of my peers. Given that most of my co-workers were much older, I felt as if I was in on a secret.

Once I began to see the upside of my new profession, I managed to get a couple of my buddies from high school to try it out. Little did I realize I had a knack for recruitment; it excited me to sell opportunity to others. In fact, I was so successful that I actually shifted the demographics in the call center.

I quickly realized that I was picking up on important real world skills. I was handling rejection on the phone every single day; I was refining a pitch; I was meeting quotas; and I was learning how to work in a professional environment. And, to think, if it weren't for that Pennysaver ad, I would have never found the job that gave me my first inside look at a Wall Street firm.

# Home of the Friars

Saint Anthony's was in a league of its own amongst Long Island high schools. Much of that was because of its highly touted football program. The allure of those Friday night games under the lights of a historic field drew in the entire community. The expectation was that our team, the Friars, would never lose. In fact, when I had arrived, they had literally been in the midst of a multi-season winning streak without a loss. There was an aura of excellence around the program, and it radiated through the halls of the school. If you wore that black–and–gold jersey on a Friday, you stood out. Although most of our team sports excelled, wearing that football jersey superseded anything else.

We were the Friars, and proud of the tradition the team upheld. When I started high school, I'd never considered playing football. I simply wasn't built for it. I had very little muscle mass; I didn't spent much time in the weight room. Given my speed on the basketball court, I could only imagine it was worse with the additional weight of shoulder pads and a helmet. No coach would be thrilled by that.

Despite those factors, I was roped in by the allure. Never did I think that I'd want to be part of a team so badly simply to become a part of the culture. In the past, I wanted to make the basketball team in order to become a better basketball player. But this was different. I wanted that jersey, and the pride of wearing it. I wanted to be with those guys, even though if one tackle went wrong I'd likely find myself in the emergency room.

High school football teams generally have big rosters, especially when most players did not play both offense and defense. Also, the bench was pretty deep, meaning that each position had a number of players waiting to get some game time. An average guy (say, for example, me) might be able to fly under the radar. I could make the team, not worry about taking massive hits on game day, and still be a part of the camaraderie in the locker room.

That was my thought process as I decided to try out for the JV team my sophomore year: an average player sitting on the bench, but still wearing that coveted jersey. As it turned out, I wasn't average when it came to football. I stunk. I got cut during tryouts, and this was a team that never cut anyone. That wasn't easy to swallow. But, deep down, I knew I wasn't built for the gridiron.

Upon reflection, I realized that I'd been cut from most of the teams that I tried out for. However, in this case, the difference was that I was expecting it; I had no experience playing football. I'd never put on a helmet and pads before; I'd never felt the grueling intensity of two-a-days under the summer sun. On the bright side, I could catch a football. But even that modest ability slipped away the first time I had a two–hundred–pound linebacker run at me.

I accepted the fact that, if I really wanted that jersey, it wasn't going to come easy. I wrestled with the demon of remembering all the countless days and nights I spent trying to be a better basketball player. All dribbling and free throws by myself out on the driveway, and then I never got a shot to play on an elite team. I thought of the promise I made to myself post-surgery: to never quit. I didn't want to do that because it felt too early to walk away.

My junior year I tried again. I was more confident this time, and blocked off those last two weeks of August, in my mind, as a time for redemption. Moreover, I was in better shape, thanks to hours spent in the weight room. Only two hurdles stood in my way: I was still not strong enough, and I couldn't take a hit. On the very first day of tryouts, I learned how little I had changed. The pounding of those summer workouts, combined with the fact that I felt like a boy among men, took a toll on me physically and mentally.

Most of my friends played contact sports all their lives. I figured that this has to be something you adjust to at a younger age, not at fifteen. The years when I was undergoing treatment and even those spent in recovery, I could never have sustained the wear and tear of a sport like football. Suddenly, a resentment filled me; I had a new chip on my shoulder. This was no longer about making the team, it was about catching up with everybody else. Even though I had my share of setbacks in life, I had to put the excuses aside. I needed to prove to myself—and anyone who would listen—that my goal was obtainable. After failing twice, I had to dig deep inside. I would not be deterred. I was not going to let my prior setbacks define me as a weak, slow, not–built–for–this–kind–of–sport kid.

\*

Another year passed. As summer approached, thankfully, I had put the SATs behind me. Socially, I had a solid footing as well. It felt as if things were coming together. I kept showing up in the weight room, though—when it came to bench presses and squat racks—I wasn't where I wanted to be, but I was noticeably in better shape. I felt more comfortable putting on those pads, ready for the morning and afternoon workouts. Most importantly, the guys on the team, knowing the work I had put in, were rooting for me this time.

After three long weeks of tryouts, the roster finally came out: I was on it! I did it. The coach gave me a pat on the back. A few days later I held it in my hands, that jersey that I gushed over for years. It was the first time I had ever made a Varsity team. And this wasn't just any team, it was perhaps the top contender in the state.

Our first pre-season game was against Don Bosco Prep, and it was going to be televised. Everyone in the community felt the buzz. All eyes were on this game. The Ironman as Don Bosco is known was a powerhouse in New Jersey (and still is). This would be a test for Saint Anthony's program which had won four consecutive CHSFL (Catholic High School Football League) Championships. Given the media spotlight, I had little expectation of playing at all. Several of my teammates were pursuing collegiate careers; they're the ones who deserved the chance to shine.

Then the big day arrived. It was a crisp late summer night, and the stadium was lit up like a scene from *Friday Night Lights*. I remember the electricity in the locker room as Coach Reichert gave his pre-game speech. I walked out of there for the very first time and proudly ran onto the freshly-cut field with my teammates. Immediately upon making a turn, I tripped over myself, falling flat on my face. Full of energy, I never popped up so quickly, looking around to see if anyone had witnessed my stumble.

The game started off slow with Don Bosco taking an early lead, but as time went on they outplayed us. They were clearly in control. We were down to the last minute of the game, and—since it was only pre-season—the coaching staff saw an opportunity to test out the other players in their rotations.

"Bishoy! Get in there! Cornerback!" the coach yelled.

Yep, my name was called. I was terrified and excited at the same time. I ran onto the field and I lined up against Don Bosco's tight end. He was fifty pounds heavier than I was, and it was definitely fifty pounds of solid muscle.

The whistle blew, and the ball was snapped. Before I knew what was happening, the tight end ran straight at me. He picked me up by the chest, and sent me airborne; I soared across the field like a bird. I'm serious. A friend of mine saw it on TV. He said it was impressive work by the cameraman to catch the entire thing, as I flew from one side of the screen to the other. After that less than impressive debut, I assumed it would be some time before my name was called again. I didn't care; it was such a rush just to be with my friends. It meant the world to me to be a the huddle, to feel the emotion in the locker room after a game.

Later that season, there was one practice where I felt wired with energy as if I had drunk three cold brews beforehand. I had a few strong tackles, which must have been perceived as uncharacteristic. The coach called me over and asked me to break down the chant in the huddle. I nodded enthusiastically. I summoned the beast within me, yelling as loud as I ever had in my life.

"Friars On Three! FRIARS ON THREE! ONE! TWO! THREE!"

I felt like a true member of the team. I had earned my jersey. Yes, it was a small win, but my confidence soared. At that moment, I realized that if I maintained my focus on a goal, I could attain it. I could attain anything. Unbeknownst to me, that experience was only setting the stage for the future.

# A Blistery Walk Across Campus

I loved my senior year of high school. I was coasting my way through academically; I had surrounded myself with a good group of friends, and I had very little worries. I took pride in my Long Island roots: our delis, our pizza, our beaches (Cooper Beach in Southampton is still my go-to), and, of course, Billy Joel.

I was not overly stressed about my future. In fact, I was open to exploring a variety of routes. I applied to fifteen colleges and got accepted into thirteen of them. I knew I wanted to move away for the experience of living on my own, but— for my parents' sake—I also wanted to be conscientious of the costs.

On a warm April day, I visited SUNY Geneseo, a New York state school. To be honest, I didn't know much about the school or the western New York region for that matter. For Long Islanders, anything above Westchester was referred to as 'upstate New York.' The scenery at Geneseo was rather distinguished; the campus overlooked a majestic valley—greenery was all around.

Academically, Geneseo had a very solid reputation; it was touted as 'the Harvard of the SUNYs,' and I had been accepted into a competitive medical program. It seemed like a 'no brainer.' My folks and I agreed that it was a win for everyone.

Growing up on Long Island, there was a sense of shelter, a pace of life associated with the place that isn't necessarily reflected by the rest of the state. We had that New York City hustle, but we also loved our laid-back summers on the beach. I didn't realize the culture shock that I was in for by simply moving to western New York. Once I got up to Geneseo for my first semester, I learned very quickly that the neighboring major cities of Rochester, Buffalo, and Syracuse were a far cry from what I was used to.

Again, I felt as if I didn't fit in, and that the social setting was drastically different. The truth is that, in high school, there was a certain type of homogeneity across the majority of students that I grew up with; they shared many of the same values.

Geneseo, on the other hand, was tremendously diverse. I felt a little exposed. I was used to everyone sharing similar core values and beliefs, going to the same places, and laughing at the same jokes. During my first two years there, I seriously considered leaving; I almost transferred to a school in Connecticut much closer to home.

In hindsight, though, I'm glad that I fought through my insecurities. I experienced several situations that I needed for my own personal growth. I needed to understand how people thought differently; I needed to hear my ideas rejected; I needed to exit my beloved comfort zone. College taught me to embrace diversity—not just cultural, but diversity in opinion. I needed that adjustment period to test my durability outside of my bubble.

Western New Yorkers are people with a work-hard, family-first, community-centered attitude. I'm lucky for all of the friends I've made there, and for the lessons I've learned. Folks up there might be a little delirious when it comes to their sports teams (I'm looking at you, Buffalo), but you have to respect their passion and their pride.

As I mentioned earlier, I was accepted into a medical program. I jumped on it because I understood it was a good opportunity, but I knew in my heart that I had no passion for medicine or biology or another ten years of education. My parents didn't push too hard; they just wanted to me to formulate a plan of attack for my future.

At the end of my freshman year, I made the conscious decision to leave the medical program and change my major to pursue a career in finance. Making the initial decision was the easy part. However, I didn't know I was about to get on the 'local route' to my career. Geneseo had no 'express' path to investment banking like some of the schools my friends attended. In fact, they did not have a formal Finance major at all. So, instead, I chose Accounting. I didn't put much weight on the specifics at the time because I was relieved to finally pursue a field I cared about.

Aside from lacking passion toward medicine, my grades were nothing to write home about. I needed a change of scenery to boost my overall profile. In the midst of a turbulent first year of college academically, this was one of the highlights. I was taking my future into my own hands; it was exciting and scary at the same time.

*

The summer before college, I was at a house party with friends. This was one of those classic parties, like something out of a movie. We were at a beautiful house around a pool on a warm summer evening. That night, through mutual acquaintances, I met a group of people from the next town over.

One of the guys, named Kenny, was also headed to Geneseo, so we exchanged information, and played a round of beer pong. I didn't think much about it again. Lo and behold, as the semester was set to start and my parents are helping me move in, guess who's checking in to the room right next door: it's Kenny. Funny how that happened. He is now one of my closest friends.

Over my freshman year, Kenny and I built a high level of trust, sharing stories about our backgrounds and the various obstacles we've had to overcome. He lost his father to cancer at a young age. Because of that tragedy, Kenny too grew up fast in his own right. The two of us clicked right away.

He'd been recruited to play soccer, and he introduced me to his teammates like I was his brother. Over the years they became like family. In fact, the first time I walked into the 'soccer house' where all his teammates lived, he told me that so long as I'm here I am a teammate. By the end of college, there were some people out there who probably thought I actually played soccer.

I'll never forget the day when I knew I was putting the idea of a medical career behind me, I celebrated my freedom when I learned that I barely passed a biology class. I ran into Kenny's dorm room and the shots were flowing; we had ourselves quite a night. Over the four years, Kenny guided me as I navigated personal issues across relationships, family, and my future. He was always selfless and went out of his way to make me feel like I belonged.

I was pumped when he asked me to give a speech at his wedding years later; I had been waiting for years to tell the world how good of a dude he was.

*

Freshman year wrapped up, and my mind was pacing on account of a few things. I was excited for summer back home in Long Island where everything would be normal again. I was ready to catch up with old friends, to eat real bagels as opposed to the pseudo–bread product served in Geneseo bakeries. And, probably best of all, I was excited to go back to the beach and all of our local spots.

Beyond that, because I decided to change majors and wanted to play catch-up, I leveraged my dad's network to get an internship at a financial institution in New York. It was unpaid, but at least it would give me a few line items on my resume. I was very grateful that he was able to make it happen.

Lastly, I was anxious about what that first year of college did to my body. I had put on nearly twenty pounds. I weighed in over 190 pounds for the first time in my life, and it wasn't muscle. It turns out the impressive collection of beer caps in my room translated into the not so remarkable gut I had amassed.

I've had ups and downs with weight as a child (at one point, I was pegged with the nickname 'Turkey' because of the rolls under my neck). But, at that time, the cause was usually my treatment. Typically, once I was off whatever medication I'd been given, I would shed the extra weight naturally.

In high school, I'd been active almost daily. I strove to build strength, but my weight was not a concern. I was never trying to be an Adonis; I just wanted to feel healthy. But that summer after my first year of college, for the first time post-treatment, I didn't look or feel good. And it was one-hundred-percent self-induced. That moment of realization was a critical juncture; I had to decide if I was going to address the issue or not.

Upon securing that internship, I reached out to my friend Riad, who was attending law school at the time in Manhattan. I told him that I would be in the city frequently and that we should catch up since we hadn't seen each other for some time. To my surprise, he told me that his roommate recently had moved out; there was a free extra bed in his apartment right by Union Square. He suggested that I use it during the week to soften the commute, and I jumped at the opportunity. I had never considered living in Manhattan, given that rents were at an all-time high, and I had no income. I had never lived in a metropolis before. I grew up in the suburbs, and my college felt like it was in the boondocks. I was a little intimidated by the city.

Aside from the fact that I knew this would cut down my travel time, I subconsciously was looking for an influence like Riad to help me address my weight gain. Riad was extremely structured, especially when it came to his workout regimen. I hadn't been exposed to discipline around my fitness since football season ended my senior year of high school; I was craving the return of a routine. I thought I could get away with staying mildly active and, clearly, I failed. A part of me recognized I would need help.

I was seeking external guidance from someone who could take me under his or her wing, and Riad was the perfect fit. I told him that I'd take him up on the offer, but only if he would hold me accountable to working out and eating right. Without hesitation, he agreed. Riad lived for that kind of challenge.

We got to work right away. He warned me that it wouldn't be easy, that I would perhaps want to quit at times, but he stressed that consistency was critical. He emphasized the importance of building patterns. To see a change, I'd have to incorporate a culmination of new habits around both my workouts and my diet. Some rapid and easy modifications included cutting out beer, soda, and sugar while increasing my water intake.

Riad proceeded to take me to his gym, where I was able to get a student discount. We set up daily workout programs, focusing on different muscle areas. I quickly found myself getting sore in places that I'd never felt before. He assured me that's how I would know that the process was kicking in.

Beyond the daily workouts, Riad preached good habits. He encouraged me to walk to and from work when possible; he guided me on my lunch orders, helping me replace sandwiches with salads loaded with protein. At night, we'd make trips to the grocery store; Riad not only showed me easy-to-incorporate recipes, but he also helped me to moderate my portions.

After a few weeks, I started to get the hang of things. I was feeling terrific. I went to the gym on my own at lunchtime. I was walking everywhere around the city. If I were at a social event, I would pass on ordering the beer and instead opt for a vodka/soda. The Fourth of July came and went. It had been six weeks since we started the program, and I weighed in for the first time. To my delight, I was down ten pounds.

I'm the type of person that doubles down on a formula if it works. So, once I saw the results, I realized I have plenty of room to improve. I figured that, if I stay focused, I could shed another ten and get back to where I was a year prior. Riad was always in my ear, telling me that he had nothing to do with the results, that it was within me all along. Even though I didn't believe him entirely, I decided to zone in and stay focused on taking small steps for the rest of the summer.

By the time my internship ended, and school was about to start back up, I found myself in the best shape of my life. Beyond the fact that I looked good and felt accomplished, my daily regime had unleashed a confidence level I never knew existed when it came to my body and what it was capable of. At nearly twenty years old, that was a powerful revelation.

I learned a few important things that summer. I learned the importance of surrounding yourself with positive influences and actively seeking them out. I learned that little actions added up and bad habits turn into patterns. I also learned about the importance of trusting the process. So, when I went back up to school, rest assured I did not return to my old ways.

Riad had warned me that it wouldn't be easy, but I had no idea what I was getting into. There were early mornings, there were cravings that I had to push back on, there were moments of doubt, but I kept my mind focused on the initial result after that first weigh-in and that drove me for a long time after—believing I can transform myself if I put my head down and get to work.

*

Now that I found some grounding when it came to my health and wellness, I quickly shifted gears back to my career prospects. Ever since Kyle gave me a glimpse of what life on Wall Street might look like back when I was in high school, I was allured by the industry. During my later years at Geneseo, it became my primary focus to navigate myself into the financial field. It would be much easier said than done, because historically Geneseo had no links to any of the investment banks or asset managers, and certainly no ties to any of the major institutions in New York City.

I told some of my friends about my plans, and although most were supportive, others tried to knock some sense into me telling me I'm in the wrong place for that. I was never concerned by the naysayers who suggested I was setting myself up for failure by pursuing this kind of career from a school that doesn't produce bankers. I took it on as yet another obstacle.

At times I'll admit I was a little delusional, but I firmly believed that all it takes to get a job in any given field is just the right introduction. I was realistic; I wasn't expecting a JP Morgan or Goldman Sachs to all of a sudden show up on campus and begin recruiting. I did, however, figure that there had to be someone in my growing network that could simply make an introduction, and I was confident (perhaps overconfident) that I could handle the rest.

I was set to graduate in May, 2009, and in the months leading up to graduation, headlines had been dominated by economic fears. It appeared we were headed toward a devastating global recession—the first of my lifetime.

I kept up with the news, but I brushed off the overall impact. If the world's top economists were unsure of the severity, then I certainly was in no place to panic; I had to be optimistic about my job prospects. I never considered the situation to be so dire that it would affect me directly, let alone an entire generation of graduates for years to come.

I carried on with my life, enjoying my last few months with the guys up at school, gearing up for spring break to roll around. We were headed down to Florida for the week. I was being proactive by applying to jobs and attending networking events, trying to gauge different opportunities. Not much was clicking, but I still wasn't discouraged. I was hoping I'd eventually get in front of the right people. I felt like I had a good grasp on the situation, and understood that I had to remain persistent.

I decided it couldn't hurt to set up a meeting with the career counselor. I figured she might be able to provide me the name of a former alumnus, then I could do the legwork. I sent her an email and requested time on her calendar at the start of the winter semester. We set it up for a few weeks out.

I remember scratching my head because the counselor was located in a building on campus I didn't recognize (and it was, by no means, a big campus). I thought it was weird that such a critical role would be placed in an office in a less than prominent part of the school. Nonetheless, I didn't read much into it. Since it was the dead of winter it was already dark outside, and I got lost finding her office. But, eventually, I arrived and knocked on the door.

The career counselor was friendly and invited me in. I sized her up pretty quickly. She seemed like someone more prepared to talk about ways to edit my resume as opposed to someone who was going to find a landing spot for my first real job. I could tell by the difference in our respective demeanors that I was there to talk business and she was not. I got straight to it; I showed her my resume. I told her about my background, and my plan to return downstate after college. I said I wanted to move to New York City and work on Wall Street, preferably for an investment bank.

Without wincing, she looked back at me, nearly let out a giggle, and said, "Uhh, we don't do that here." My heart sank.

Even though I should have known, I had led myself to believe that it couldn't actually be the case that an accredited university, recognized for its academics, couldn't give me a phone number or an email address. I thanked her (for nothing) and walked back through the blistery chill to my apartment. I was down, and I blamed myself for it.

"Holy shit, Bishoy, you just threw away four years of your life," I thought to myself. I had regrets about deciding to stick things out instead of transferring when I had the chance.

The world was in the midst of a massive recession, I had no employment lined up after college. As I saw it, my university failed me. The counselor basically told me not to get my hopes up about getting the job I had worked for. That cold, hard fact took a while to process. I was frustrated, questioning the path I had taken. But slowly, in the coming days, I pulled myself together.

"Bishoy, you've been here before," I thought. "You've been told the odds are against you. You've been told you wouldn't make it,. You've been told you should consider less."

I began to seek out opportunity in weakness. I knew the job market was bleak, but I also knew that if anyone could apply patience in his quest it would be me. I knew I needed to maintain my perspective. No one was going to call out of the blue and offer me a position, especially considering the thousands of applications from all of the other students across the country competing for employment during this difficult crisis. I had to get tactical; I had to take steps and build myself up.

I tasked myself with filling the gaps that Geneseo was unable to provide. I had to summon strength in what felt like a moment of despair. There was only so much negativity I could feed myself before I came to the moment of realization that "I've been here before" and that was the moment I began my professional journey.

# You Don't Meet People by Accident

# The Pennysaver

After graduation, I moved back to Long Island, and it didn't take long for that positive self-talk to quickly wear off. I had come to accept the cards as they had been dealt. I was confident that I was qualified; but frustrated that somehow here I was stuck at mom and dad's house with a college degree and nothing to show for it.

I questioned universal law. I felt as though I had to prove myself yet again. After everything I had persevered through—proving I could battle disease, that I could make friends, that I could make the team—why did I need to prove that I'm qualified for gainful employment? How did I find myself in that position?

My parents took different approaches when they noticed I was down on myself. My mother would come into my room and talk strategy. She's a planner, and maps her steps. But I didn't want to hear any of it; I would find myself getting angry. I realized that I had no grasp of the situation. Employers weren't returning my emails; application portals felt like black holes. I didn't want to show her weakness. I didn't want her to know I was losing hope. I wanted to assure her that I had a plan, even though I was stewing in desperation. In those months after coming home, my stress levels spiked. At twenty-two I had grey hairs sprouting daily. I resented that I had to keep battling to earn my seat, I felt like I had the world to offer, and the universe was simply saying, "No, thanks."

My father had seen this story before. He's seen many people lose jobs and struggle to find a livelihood. He understood that there wasn't one single answer; each journey is unique, so he never gave me a set of instructions. My father's main concern was that I keep my chin up, and not rest on my laurels. Failure was okay; giving up was not. I understood that both my parents had the best intentions in mind. They maintained a balanced approach in supporting me at a time when I was losing faith in myself.

Around the middle of the summer, my father approached me. He mentioned he had talked to someone recently who was looking for a bookkeeper and asked me if I would be interested. Although I understood that there was no glamour to the position, I jumped on it; I couldn't sit at home navigating job portals on the web anymore. I couldn't stand to see the gap on my resume grow any further. I was accepted for the position, and commuted over an hour every day in traffic to get there. I was grateful for the opportunity, but the mutual understanding was that this was not going to be my career, only a step. It was on me to determine where I would go next.

Unfortunately, the impact of the recession was still stinging the employment market; unemployment was soaring. A part of me thought, "I should be happy that someone is paying me" and the other part thought, "This can't be what real life is like; I don't have a career, I have a job." There was a constant internal dilemma: I was appreciative for the opportunity, yet I feared that it was not my welcome mat to Wall Street. Yet in spite of the evidence that I was far from my destination, I refused to close the door on a dream.

It was now the winter of 2009. During the holidays, I caught up with friends and family. They shared all of their updates, and it felt like everyone was doing something, going somewhere. It forced me to a moment of self-examination, I realized that I was becoming complacent—going to work, collecting my paycheck, not doing anything to pursue my next step. When you're living at home, it's easy to settle for less because there's no rent payment looming, most of my money went towards wants not needs. Most of my life, I had operated with a sense of urgency, but now, for some reason, I lapsed. It could have been the scarring of graduating unemployed. I couldn't wrap my finger around how I let go of that fire.

A few days after New Years, at the very start of 2010, I was driving home from work. I remember the traffic was particularly nasty due to the frigid temperatures. Anyway, an ad came on the radio for the Pennysaver, the local magazine that I used to find the telemarketing gig in high school. I laughed out loud. But then, simultaneously, I had an "ah-ha" moment.

"Maybe I need to channel the Bishoy from high school," I thought. "He was scrappy."

Realistically, I didn't anticipate that I'd get a Wall Street gig from the Pennysaver, but I thought maybe I could find my next step. I had to expand my reach. I went home that night, and I pulled up the Help Wanted section in every local paper. Inside Newsday, the biggest newspaper on Long Island, I came across an opening from an Executive Search firm in the next town over.

"This job would cut my commute dramatically," I thought. "It seems to pay well. Even though I know nothing about recruiting, it will surely get me in front of some decision-makers."

I knew I needed more interaction. Working in the accounting department of a small company undoubtedly limited me on that front. So I sent in my application. A few short days later, I got invited in for an interview.

I met with the two heads of the business. Even though they were both settled down with kids, they came off as frat brothers. Given I was just a year out of college, that appealed to me. We hit it off, and I got the job. They told me the position's focus would be placing public accountants. They liked that I had some essential accounting experience and a matching degree. I was excited. This was not an hourly gig, it was a full-time job with benefits. I was moving up.

*

My boss at the bookkeeping job gave me a nod of encouragement and sent me on my way. It was the early months of 2010; I was approaching one year out of college, and relieved about the change of scenery. I needed a shakeup from the small company structure, a more corporate environment. I found it at Melville Search (not the firm's real name). The company was the search arm of the Melville CPA Group, one of the larger public accounting firms on Long Island. I realized that I had found a unique situation that allowed me to see the inner workings of a public accounting firm while operating in a completely different function.

Melville Search was not only responsible for recruiting for Melville CPA Group, it actively recruited for external clients, public and private. My role at first was simply to source resumes using a variety of platforms, primarily for accounting roles. It was pretty easy to identify a good resume; I looked at schooling, experience, and certification as well overall resume presentation (i.e., spelling and grammar). Once I found a candidate, my boss would reach out to present to them the opportunities we had in our pipeline. There's a very comprehensive skillset involved in recruiting that I didn't consider from day one. It's not as easy as matching a resume to a job description. It consists of speaking the language of the client and the candidate; it involves a keen sense of business development and industry awareness. It's not the type of job where you can "fake it till you make it;" eventually you will get exposed.

After a couple months, sourcing lost its flavor; I was beginning to see the same resumes over and over. I felt underutilized, so I asked for expanded responsibility. I started screening candidates over the phone and in-person. Soon I was actively engaged in business development, leveraging my network to get exclusive rights for Melville Search to lead searches for external parties. A friend of mine worked for a major technology company (which, at the time, was one of the ten largest firms in the industry), and he connected me with the right people on the inside. After a business dinner, the papers were signed, and we had the rights. I was excited; it was my first close. I was just 23, and it was perhaps the most significant client to engage with Melville Search.

In spite of the traction I'd made, not all was rosy. I was the youngest in the group by a long shot; my colleagues had all been in the business for several years. I was in my first corporate job, with all the energy in the world, geared toward climbing the ladder. I only knew one speed, and—even though I could sense some type of resentment—no one was going to shoot down my ambition. This was my first encounter with bureaucracy in the workplace. But, because I was full of fire, I brushed it off for as long as I could.

Around that time, I started to pick up on the reputation of the industry: good candidates had issues trusting recruiters. The fear was that recruiters did not always have the candidate's interest in mind' they only had their eyes on the placement fee. To some people, it felt like recruiters attempted to fit square pegs in round holes. I personally couldn't live with myself if I steered someone to a role that wasn't their best fit. I noticed others using sales tactics to close deals. It didn't sit well with me; it felt like the whole process should've been more consultative.

I was always pretty grounded morally and, at a young age, swore to never lie, steal, or cheat. As an adult, I applied that ethic toward closing a sale; I focused on the client's best interest. Unfortunately, at times, the recruiting culture felt like a combination of all three vices: lying, cheating, and stealing. Don't get wrong; I applaud all the honest recruiters out there. The problem, I think, often starts at the top, that's where the tone is set. When it's not, things can spiral out of control quickly. So, while the negative reputation of the recruiting industry doesn't reside everywhere, it caught me a little off guard at Melville Search.

In December 2010, after saving some money, I decided to move to Manhattan in order to work out of Melville Search's Midtown office. I thought that maybe the city would yield more and different candidates, an opportunity to expand my reach. It was an exciting change; however, after a while, the same issues surfaced. Resumes were repeating, good candidates pushed back on the roles we had to offer, management was resistant to change. Eventually, it my work felt more and more robotic. That was the beginning of the end, when I realized that this was not going to be my career. It was just another job, albeit slightly better than the last one.

Management and I had gone back and forth for a couple months around strategy and execution; we did not see eye to eye. I refused to partake in certain parts of their plan. I felt that there were instances where my better judgment was being compromised. By early spring of 2011, I was laid off. I was stunned. Getting laid off was bittersweet; it was my first time experiencing a 'break-up' like that, but it was also incredibly liberating. It was like being removed from a toxic relationship, like the universe was telling me that it had seen enough. It was time to take my talents elsewhere.

# Chasing a Cure for Charley

After getting let go from Melville Search, I had to act quick as there wasn't much time for soul searching. It was either find a job or face the reality of moving back home, and, at all costs, I was going to avoid that option. The very thought of it, at age 23, signified failure. It reinvigorated those thoughts I had after graduation that there was no place for me in the workforce. Moving in with my parents would take me two steps backward on what felt like a no-end-in-sight trek to Wall Street.

In spite of the circumstances, I managed to cultivate peace of mind around the relationships I had built during my time at Melville Search. I had been engaged with decision-makers at client firms, and maintained good standing with senior leaders at Melville CPA Group.

I was looking for public accounting gigs at this point. I figured it was time to leverage my degree and—given I had an inside look at Melville—I knew what to expect in terms of the work, the culture, and the hours. I understood I would have to be crafty if I took on a role at a public accounting firm because it is rather easy to get sucked in. There is no shortage of work, and no managers walking around the office telling you to stop billing clients. The more billable hours, the better. I also knew that I could get cornered into a career that I wasn't passionate about. I was conscientious of that during my search, thinking of ways to gain employment and not put myself in a position where I would become a slave to a firm that most likely wouldn't reciprocate.

About a month into the search, I attended a charity event at Casa La Femme, by far the most trendy Egyptian bar/restaurant in the city. The event was to raise money for an orphanage being built in Egypt. I was familiar with most faces in the crowd. Historically at these events, substantial donors in the business community attend. I figured it would be good for me to mingle in hopes of snagging a business card. After a few cocktails, I was feeling loose. A friend asked me how work was going, I told her what happened, and she turned right behind her tapped on a gentleman's shoulder.

"Bishoy meet John. John, I think you can help him."

I told John about my situation. Even though he may have had more to drink than I did up to that point, without hesitation, John said he would help me out. He asked me to send him a resume. He told me that his dad, Nabil, was a controller at one of the more recognized city clubs and had a great relationship with a firm in lower Manhattan. John was smooth, he also was a straight shooter. I felt like I was in the right hands.

The next day I got an email from John. He said he passed my resume to his father. Within days, I got a call from a firm known as Condon O'Meara McGinty and Donnelly (COMD); they invited me to interview with a partner.

I had no public accounting experience, and wasn't in a position to brag about my grades; they were average. I had to sell myself on being a hard-working, dedicated, and responsible professional. I got to the interview, and the partner asked me how I knew Nabil. Per John's instructions, I said that Nabil is my uncle. The partner looked at me, and smiled, "Well, we love Nabil here." He proceeded to ask me a few general questions about my background. I walked out of there thinking, "Well, that was easy."

Within the same week, I received an offer from COMD. I was ecstatic; I accepted right away. I wasn't going to have to move home; I was going to make more money than my last role; and I was going to embark on a new challenge. I called John to let him know. I told him that I had to meet his dad at any cost; I wanted to thank him in person. I knew full well that he was the only reason I got that job, and I needed to understand why he invested in me.

I met Nabil for lunch at his club. He sat me down in his office. With my excitement apparent, I thanked him. He smiled.

"John told me about you," he said. "He knows your father and spoke very highly of his kindness. I like to reward kindness with kindness."

I'm never surprised when an Egyptian mentions they know my father; he has a pretty broad reach. I was thankful that my father's reputation helped me get an opportunity when I needed one. I asked Nabil if he had any advice before I start at COMD. He pulled his chair up to the desk; his face became stern.

"I don't care what you do ultimately," he said. "I don't care if you become a partner, or if you decide to turn in your calculator and become the janitor. All I care about is that what you choose to do, you do it well. That you become the *best* at it. That you distinguish yourself from the pack."

My father is savvy when it comes to management. However, he has never worked for or managed a business in his adult life. Sure, the church involves oversight, and it takes keen business sense to keep things running smoothly, but there are differences. For the first time in my life, a person was guiding me in the realm of business. In a very fatherly way, Nabil saw me as a son; he spoke to me the way he talked to John. He believed in me. I found solace in Nabil's guidance; I was not going to let him down.

I told Nabil that, ultimately, I wanted to make it on Wall Street. His eyes lit up. He said to focus on what I have in front of me and, in due time, that door will open. I loved that he didn't push back on my dream out of fear that I would jump ship on a firm that he had just referred me to.

Full of positivity, I went home and I submitted applications for part-time MBA programs. I gazed at myself in the mirror and made a promise that the year ahead was going to be the most rigorous one of my professional career. If I stayed true to Nabil's guidance, it would pay off. I got accepted into Fordham University's program in May of 2011. Between work and school, I was either going to sink or swim and, quite frankly, sinking was not an option.

\*

Over that summer, I wrapped my head around learning the day-to-day responsibilities of being an auditor. I was observing the stark contrast between what you are taught in textbooks versus daily application. It was a relief of sorts because books put me to sleep. However, once I was in the weeds on a financial statement, I found myself engaged. COMD was traditional in the sense that almost everything was done by hand; they had yet to move to a digital platform. Even if it wasn't efficient, working in an 'analog' realm paid dividends for my learning curve.

COMD was a mid-size firm. The staff accountants were tasked with general duties around each client as opposed to larger firms where the function is more specialized. The firm was focused on not-for-profit entities, including private city clubs and country clubs (for instance, the Harvard Club). The people I had come to meet were all amiable; the office had a family feel to it. I quickly learned that this was a direct result of the long hours. If you're going to be spending a lot of time with your co-workers, it should be a welcoming environment.

I was set to start my MBA at the Gabelli School of Business at Fordham in August, so I did my best to enjoy the early months of summer before buckling down. To be honest, I was unsure if taking on a new job and diving into an intense graduate program simultaneously would burn me out. I was also unsure if Fordham's price tag was justified. I had never spent six figures on anything. This was the most expensive 'investment' I had ever made.

As summer continued, I prepared to go into hiding. I needed to show myself that I had grit, no matter the sacrifice. Whether it was time with family, friends, or my workouts, I had to prove that I could give my all professionally in hopes of reaping a reward. I was testing the whole 'hard work pays off' mantra.

A highlight of enrolling at Fordham was the emphasis on the accommodations provided for part-time students. The scheduling was friendly; the sessions were lightly catered; and the professors were considerate of business travel arrangements. That really played to my favor. I went into the semester ready to put my head down and do what I had to do in order to succeed academically. I wasn't there to make friends, I was there to get those three letters, and leverage them to find a spot on Wall Street. I was sitting amongst students that all worked for major institutions, why couldn't that be me? I felt as though I was inching closer to my goal.

Back at my job, after successfully working a few engagements, I had demonstrated to management that I was capable of taking on more, and was given individual commitments to oversee. I'd be responsible for the presentation of client's financial statements for the year. It was rewarding to gain management's trust at such a young age. I wanted any responsibility that I could get my hand on.

One of my first clients was a not-for-profit called Charley's Fund. The organization was named after Charley, a young boy who was diagnosed with Duchenne Muscular Dystrophy (DMD), which caught his family by surprise. His mother, Tracy, started the charity to accelerate the government approval of a treatment for her son's debilitating diagnosis. I had never heard of DMD before. There were pictures of Charley all over the office; he looked like your typical middle school student, with a radiant smile in every photo. For someone facing a deadly disease, he seemed like the type of child who lit up a room. In talking to Tracy, I understood her unrelenting passion and sense of urgency for the cause. I was able to draw parallels between her mission and the plight my parents faced when I was younger. In the face of disease, parents will stop at nothing to fight for their child's recovery. She and I bonded over this shared sense of purpose.

From my seat as an auditor, Tracy was far from what you might call a 'good client.' Her relentless mission was to find a cure; the non-profit's paperwork and bookkeeping was secondary. I caught myself coming off as insensitive because I wanted to complete the engagement in a timely fashion. I was frustrated that the files were not in order. Yet, after a day–long chat in her small office, I couldn't help but shift gears. I left with nothing but the utmost respect for a woman who devoted her life to her son's trying disease.

I met Tracy at a crucial point during the first semester of my MBA; I was reaching a place of burnout. To make it to my class, I commuted from the Berkshires to New York City three times in one week. My days started at six in the morning; I finished class at ten at night; then I drove for three hours back to my hotel room.

Tracy didn't know it, but she helped me keep perspective at a time when I was running on fumes. She put everything into Charley's Fund. She executed purposefully in the face of many tribulations, and that inspired me to keep pushing forward, even when I had no idea if my efforts would ever pay off. I was pursuing a career while she was chasing a cure.

# Silver Jubilee

Just after Labor Day that year, COMD hired six new accountants, all of whom were young like me—full of energy with a desire to hit the ground running. It was timely as we were approaching a busy season, and simultaneously had an upcoming peer review, which is a periodic external review of COMD's quality control system. It's executed to ensure the firm is employing best practices.

At this point, I had been with the firm for about four months, and—although my output was reliable and feedback positive—I hadn't done much to stand out. Around this time, I noticed that management was bogged down with deadlines. They certainly had no time to train new staff, so I thought perhaps I could alleviate some of the burdens of the peer review.

I took it upon myself to delegate the work amongst the new staff. I bounced around from desk to desk, giving instructions and answering questions. I wasn't entirely sure if what I was doing was kosher. I waited for someone from management to remind me that I wasn't in a position to be undertaking such a project. The new staff was appreciative of the help, and a partner pulled me into his office to thank me for employing a sense of urgency amid endless deliverables. I tested the boundaries, and it ended up playing out in my favor. As a result, I was given more responsibility. This made me feel good about my relationship with management at COMD. They trusted me. I felt like I was finding my footing professionally.

I remembered the advice Nabil gave me.

"I don't care what you do ultimately. I don't care if you become a partner, or if you decide to turn in your calculator and become the janitor. All I care is that what you choose to do, you do it well. That you become the *best* at it."

At that moment, I felt as though I had made Nabil proud. Though I was only a few months into the seat and no expert, I was a hard worker.

Once peer reviews were completed, I was able to breathe a little. I got up to speed on everything at school and, I hate to admit it, finally pay more attention to the things that really mattered in my life, like family. November marked the twenty-fifth anniversary of my father's ordination as a priest. He was never one for celebrations or attention, so he did his best to downplay any extra noise around the event. My father didn't want congregants spending much on him, he'd prefer they make charitable donations to those in need. He didn't want anyone to burden themself for a celebration. Instead of setting up a party at an external venue, he requested that any event be held at the church, that any meals be served in the church hall. The planners obliged, and a date was set.

It was an interesting dynamic. On the one hand, there was a buzz; people wanted to acknowledge his dedication to service. On the other hand, at home, he downplayed the significance. I'd find myself conflicted, wondering if the event was a big deal or not. Yet, in any case, I wasn't going to miss it; I was proud of him.

My father puts his every waking hour into his service, and most of those hours he works behind the scenes tackling some of the most distressful situations that only few could fathom. He does his job with an overwhelming grace, making it look easy and somehow keeping his emotions stable. He may be exhausted emotionally at times, but his support tank never appears to be empty.

One of the members of the planning committee reached out to me, asking if there were any folks, beyond the congregation, that they should extend an invite to. Immediately, I thought of my former principal, Brother Gary Cregan from Saint Anthony's High School. He was a Franciscan brother, a history buff, and a scholar. When he found out that my father was a Coptic Orthodox priest, he took a deep-rooted interest in me. Brother Gary knew the history of the Orthodox Church and was insistent on meeting my father. Coincidentally, the planning committee member had two daughters that were enrolled at Saint Anthony's at the time, so he was able to access Brother Gary easily.

✳

When the night of the silver jubilee came around, to my father's delight, the event was very simple. There were several speeches given by members of the Board, Sunday School teachers, and other leaders. I was sitting next to my dad, and he was his usual self, uncomfortable accepting praise of any kind. His face turned red below the beard every time someone acknowledged his work. After the speeches and a presentation by children in the congregation, a video screen descended. On it were the words, "Special Message from Brother Gary Cregan."

You have to realize that almost everyone in the church had no idea who Brother Gary was. But I knew him to be extraordinarily eloquent and well-spoken; he commands a room. Brother Gary started off by congratulating my father, then he addressed the congregation as a whole. "Among you is a saint," he said. "A man who is tireless in his devotion."

A saint? That was powerful. I looked at my dad, and I could tell he was taken with emotion. After the video ended, my father got up and took the microphone. He struggled at first to find proper words of gratitude. He thanked the entire congregation and all of the speakers. He downplayed his work, reminding the people that he is driven by those around him; any progress made is not his alone. Then he did something peculiar.

My father is very implicit in his affection. He doesn't outwardly express tenderness; he shows it with his actions. But, at that moment, he let his guard down. He thanked my mother for her unconditional love and support, reminding congregants that she is his support system. He praised my sister and I as his children, then took it one step further. He thanked me personally, and shared with the entire congregation that he was proud of me for my "strength."

Time stood still after hearing him say that.

I was only twenty-four, barely established in my personal life. It overjoyed me to get that recognition from him. Yet, at the same time, I was scratching my head. "Who me? Strong? I'm not strong, no one's ever called me that."

In fact, I always thought of myself as weak. I never characterized myself as strong physically or mentally. The world had always told me that I didn't size up. But, here was my father, proudly stating that I was the opposite: strong, not weak.

It was emotional for me to understand that my father always believed in me, even when I didn't fully believe in myself. At that moment, I was rejuvenated. I felt a spaciousness inside my chest. No matter what he thought or felt quietly in his heart, I didn't realize how much I needed to hear him actually say it out loud.

My father has witnessed life and death in all forms. He has visited the imprisoned and comforted victims of the most severe types of trauma. In the midst of all that, he was able to prioritize his family. He always kept us at the forefront, and protected our well–being on all fronts. He is a visionary, ever one step ahead, guiding us as we move forward through our lives. He shielded us from realities when they were coming at us too fast for our growth and development, but he also allowed us to fall over and over again so we could learn on our own.

My father taught me the significance of embracing failures with enthusiasm and dignity. He understood that prepared me for the opportunities that were to come my way. Every single rejection—whether it was getting cut from a sports team, not getting a job or an interview, or even getting my heart shattered—he always had the same reaction. With a calming delivery, he'd say, "It's okay, everything is going to work out." To this day, I never question him because, to this day, everything has worked out.

# It's Not About What You Know, It's About Who You Know

# The Morning-After Text

My first winter rolled around at COMD and colleagues were encouraging me to enjoy the holidays because, they said, once January came around, we'd hit the pavement for busy season. They said to expect tight deadlines, cranky partners, long nights, and lots of Seamless in my diet. They painted a bleak picture, yet I was looking forward to the 'misery.' The way I saw it, it was game time.

"How bad do I want to succeed?" I thought. "How much am I willing to sacrifice to show myself and others that I belong on this playing field?"

For the next four months, my sleep schedule was non-existent; I worked through the night on multiple occasions. My diet consisted of black coffee, fruit, and yogurt. I was wired, but I had no regrets. I was unapologetic around the fact that I hadn't been home to visit my parents for a couple months, and that I haven't been in touch with my friends. My roommate Farrell got used to the lights in our apartment coming on at weird hours when I came home.

Truth be told, I doubled down on my burden those months by enrolling in five classes that semester. I wanted to get through my MBA as soon as possible. I figured that the sooner I finished, the sooner I'd be positioned for a gig on Wall Street. By April of the next year (2012), the busy season was winding down; finals were approaching; I began to see daylight. At my job, management had started focusing on summer assignments. I was asked to work on the firm's most significant account. Typically, a client like this was assigned to designated staff as a recognition of their work during the busy season. It was another affirmative nod from management; it felt good to be appreciated.

However, though positive for me in the short term, getting the assignment was bittersweet. In the grander picture, I was becoming anxious that I was, perhaps, cementing myself too deeply in the world of public accounting. It was not sustainable for the rest of my career. I couldn't imagine putting my self, or my future family, through four months of endless work every year. Looking around at the folks who'd been in the industry for a long time, it was clear that the job took a toll.

In those weeks, I was invited to my friend Chris' birthday party at a dive bar in the Lower East Side of Manhattan. I acknowledged I had been a subpar friend, and I made it a point to go, even though I needed a couple extra hours of sleep. It was a warm spring night, and the bar was lively that evening; the boys were in good spirits.

My friends, for the most part, were working jobs in the fields they pursued. They had time to live balanced lives, to exercise, to date, to experience New York for all it had to offer. Once again, I felt like the odd man out.

After having a few drinks, a friend named Mike (who goes by the name Ervo), that I had not seen in a while, asked me about work. I held nothing back. I told him how I felt uncertain about my journey; how the hours were grueling; how I juggled work and school and thought it may not pay off; how I didn't understand how others seemed to have it figured out while I was always pushing.

After listening to me ramble, Ervo asked me to send him my resume. As with most conversations that begin in the wee hours of the morning after several rounds, I didn't take him too seriously. The next morning I woke up with a painful hangover, and a text message from Ervo, "Hey man, you never sent me your resume."

I was stunned.

Let's think about this for a moment. I networked my tail off over that year, meeting with directors, managers, and decision makers that said they would "keep me in mind" for openings. Then, all of a sudden, here was a twenty-five-year-old buddy with a junior title who went the extra mile when he didn't have to.

I was cautiously optimistic. It helped that he seemed confident he could make things happen. I realize now that it's always about *who* you know as opposed to *what* you know. My advice is to take the time to talk to the people around you. Prepare to give before you ever anticipate receiving. When I talked with Ervo, it was an opportunity to blow off steam. I expected nothing from that night.

*

Two weeks went by, and I didn't hear back from him. Yet, for some reason, I still felt optimistic. Similar to my last transition, I had given my all, and I felt the universe heard me. I texted Ervo, and he said he was on it. Shortly after I got a call from a hiring manager at a premier investment bank. The manager said he was handed my resume and wanted to talk to me. I found out later that Ervo sat right next to him. The manager sent over the job description, and we scheduled an in-person interview. I glazed over the requirements, and lost all my momentum. My background was a far cry from the bullet points on that document. Why would they bother with a guy with no transferable experience?

At that time, I was auditing not-for-profit city clubs and country clubs. The role at the investment bank was for a seat on the desk that managed risk for interest rate derivatives.

"What the hell is an interest rate derivative?" I wondered.

It sounded sexy, but I had no business getting that role over anyone else. I didn't know the first thing about the actual job. If they asked me the most basic technical question, I'd be toast.

Ervo offered to prepare me before my interview. He told me to leverage my soft skills. He reassured me there was a reason he didn't hesitate to pass along my resume. So I studied up. If they didn't ask many questions, I'd be able to get by and sound competent.

I remember walking into the building—383 Madison Ave, the former Bear Stearns building. There was a gloomy feel to the lobby, a historic vibe seeping through the architecture. I took the elevator up to the twenty-sixth floor. It was my first time seeing a trading desk set-up. I started picturing myself in one of those seats.

I sat down in the conference room. The hiring manager came in, and shook my hand. I could tell right away he was more of an introvert. He gave me a quick background on his role and the team he managed. As I watched his mannerisms, I knew I was sitting in front of a very bright individual. I picked up on the fact that he was unlikely to dominate the dialogue. I needed to say enough (without shooting myself in the foot) to get on his good side.

I asked him where he grew up. He mentioned that he attended Chaminade High School, which happened to be Saint Anthony's biggest rival. That helped me break the ice. I was able to avoid talking about the technical stuff that I still barely understood.

As the clock ticked, he shifted gears toward my motives. Why did I want this role? I drew parallels between how I could translate success from my current position into success with the bank. It may have been the most significant stretch in interview history.

I left the office thinking it could have gone in either direction. I didn't do anything overly critical, but I certainly didn't blow anyone away with my technical skillset. To be honest, I'm not sure if he bought what I was saying in the interview, or if he simply trusted Ervo's recommendation.

A few weeks went by. It was now June. Then I got a phone call, and an offer. After three years of clawing, scratching, and stretching myself, I was finally invited to join the ranks on Wall Street. I made it into the industry as an analyst at JP Morgan. Damn, it felt good.

I called my father, and he was very excited. As is always the case, I felt like he knew this was just a matter of time. I also called Nabil and set up a lunch with him. His enthusiasm was beyond words. He reminded me of his original words of advice, and suggested that I celebrate this new milestone.

# Penn Station is Not a Tourist Attraction

My first six months at JP Morgan were a bit overwhelming, to say the least. Every time I walked into the lobby, a lobby that is a staple on CNBC and Bloomberg TV, I would question how I ever made it in. I felt like I had everybody fooled including myself.

Looking around the floor, seeing all the big computer terminals, made me chuckle about how COMD had yet to go paperless; here I was sitting in front of a $25,000 machine. I felt like I was holding on to a secret for dear life. The secret was I had no idea what was going on when it came to my actual job; I was just following instructions. I was afraid of being exposed. I'd been hired to work on one of the most sophisticated trading desks in the bank, and that realization made my stomach turn.

In those initial weeks, I did plenty of nodding and note-taking, but I hardly retained again. I did my best not let on that I was lost. I was in over my head, working with people who could double as human calculators. Seriously, my colleagues did mental math that I couldn't navigate with all the technology at my disposal.

The thing about traders at a big investment bank like JP Morgan is that they operate at lightning speed. I needed to work closely with a group fo them. It wasn't merely good enough for me to understand what they were doing behind those investment models, they needed me to speak their language at the same speed. Given their objective was to drive revenue for the firm, they had no time to hold someone's hand or teach them from scratch.

I revisited Nabil's advice. Amongst these titans, I was unlikely to become the *best* at navigating interest rate derivatives and options math, so I wasn't going to bother with that. I did, however, uncover an area of opportunity. I realized that if there's one thing I could do well it was to communicate with other. And, because of the chaos of the trading day, communication can be weak in a firm that size.

"Okay, Bishoy," I thought. "Who cares if you can communicate? That doesn't help anyone's bottom line."

But I ignored my inner critic, and became convinced that there was a problem to solve. Given we were working with such complex products, it would probably be helpful to the overall business if someone (like myself) figured out a way to simplify the story, and talk in laymen's terms, so that the next analyst who came in didn't find themselves head-scratching for months.

Over the next year or so, I ramped up efficiency. I absorbed the context, and I was much more fluid in conversing on the floor. I worked with my team to clean up the excess complexities of some of our processes, and put together presentations intended to explain our products to the average person. There was a massive volume of dollars that got traded daily; I'm talking billions. So I figured if someone wanted to explain our products at a dining room table, they should be able to do it in an understandable fashion.

My efforts built a trusted relationship with management. They appreciated my ability to produce, and my dedication to the team. I finally I started to get comfortable for the first time since I entered JP Morgan. Tracing back to when I took the job at COMD, I had been entirely devoted to my professional footprint, to completing my MBA, to figuring out if I belonged at a bank like JP Morgan. While all that was good, it was not fulfilling. I felt a void. I felt like I'd been selfish, looking for more money and personal gain. But I wasn't giving anything back to society.

I didn't know where I belonged in the grander scheme of things. I felt like life had to be more to life than succeeding at JP Morgan. There had to be a human element to my satisfaction, it couldn't come purely from work. I thought about volunteering in one way or another to balance things out, to find a way to give back.

Around that time, I was inundated with emails from Habitat for Humanity. I'm not much of a handyman; I'd figured that I'd be more of a nuisance than a help. Then I remembered that JP Morgan had opportunities in the community, so I researched their database of volunteer programs. I found a mentorship program that paired young professionals with individual high school students. Bingo. I liked the idea of working with an individual, a young person in search of hope. I remembered how lost I was when high school began. If I could help someone build confidence, it would fill that gap for at least one person. I signed up.

*

A few weeks later I left work, still wearing my suit, and took the subway up to a Catholic high school in the Bronx. I was introduced to the student I had been assigned, Juan (not his real name). He was accompanied by his mother. Juan was a freshman, timid and soft-spoken. I had to get closer to even catch his name when he said it. After introducing myself, his mother pulled me aside.

"I need your help," she said. "Juan is co-dependent. I want him to build up his confidence and his independence. He's struggled socially. He used to get beat up by girls in middle school."

I told her I would do my best. I didn't want to let her down. This was the type of challenge I was seeking even though I had no idea how I was going to tackle it.

A few weeks went by. Juan and I had been in touch via phone but, as the holidays approached that year, I thought it would be nice to take him out in person. I knew he liked basketball, so I reached out to a friend who had Knicks season tickets and asked him if he had any games to spare. He kindly gave me a pair of tickets. Juan was thrilled. He'd never been to a professional game before. Mind you, I'd gone to games since I was a child. I had opportunities to sit courtside and in boxes. To me, the experience at Madison Square Garden is timeless. I was excited to get Juan out there.

Game day approached. Juan was going ride the subway down to Midtown to meet me near my office. If you know your way around New York City, you know that the area around Madison Square Garden isn't the most aesthetically pleasing; there's lots of traffic, mild pollution, and the homeless look for shelter all around.

As we got off the 1 Train and walked through the turnstiles, I glanced at Juan; his jaw dropped when he got to Penn Station. He was from the Bronx, and he had never been there before. To him, it was fantastic. I was taken aback. Penn Station is not a tourist attraction in the slightest. It is constantly patrolled by police officers, far from well maintained, and always under construction.

Juan was unwavering in his gratitude before we even got to the main attraction. When I asked him what he wanted to eat, he suggested getting chicken wings from Atomic Wings (again, the most basic of chains, but it's what he wanted). So we went.

I was reminded about why perspective is so crucial to a fifteen-year-old. I kept in touch with Juan frequently after that day, and I was thrilled to find out he went on to become a basketball player, graduate high school, and earn a full-ride to college.

When his mother first told me about Juan's background, I felt unworthy for that kind of undertaking. In fact, it turned out he had a more significant impact on me than, perhaps, I had on him. My experience with Juan taught me that I had a lot to learn. I wanted to give back, but I wasn't ready to be entirely selfless and invested. I balanced my professional ambition by contributing to society, but the one thing I learned about mentorship is that to reap the full rewards, it's important that I separate the two.

I was Juan's biggest cheerleader and things ended well. However, I took a pause from investing in more mentees, realizing I had to get to a point where I could give more of myself. Juan gave me perspective around investing in others, and I'm grateful for that.

# The Cardinal Rule

After a few years, in 2014, Ervo was ready to take his next step and left our team. He made the decision to see through his passions in the world of real estate. Over the previous two years, the two of us built a bond. He helped me get up to speed when I was running around like a headless chicken my first year. He understood the people dynamic, the expectations from management, and, most importantly, the limitations of the role we were in.

We worked in a middle office function and, in the financial services world, there is a segregation between back office, middle office, and front office. The front office includes sales personnel, corporate finance, and revenue-generating parts of the business; the middle office manages the risk and technology resources; and the back office focuses on administrative support. All three must work together for the business to flow, however, there was no hiding that the glory and, ultimately, the pay sat with the front office.

The sentiment across the industry in the biggest institutions (JP Morgan being one of them) is that it's challenging to transition from one office to the other. You really need to stand out to prove you are worthy of that kind of promotion. Even after you display capability, it's still tough because you are up against a world of qualified talent from the outside. It was a frustrating realization for some, myself included.

I found myself in a rut for a while because I knew that I would undoubtedly succeed in a front office function. My skill set was probably best suited for that kind of role, given my strengths were highlighted through my interactions, and not through my analytics. However, I had to overcome this ridiculous barrier that has been quietly erected within the industry over time.

I came in the door at JP Morgan because of an opening in the middle office, and because Ervo advocated for me even though there were many candidates out there who may have been better suited. But, when I tried to move into a function that was more in my wheelhouse, I felt as though I had been labeled as middle office material. I would apply to front office opportunities and find myself addressing questions such as "Given you have not dealt with clients, what makes you think you'll be able to tackle X role?"

I felt people failed to understand that client engagement is a skill honed throughout a lifetime, not one that is taught in a professional training program. You either have what it takes to engage, or you don't. You can show someone a product, but the only way a person learns how to give best-in-class service is by engagement. When it comes to working with clients, the task is simple: find out what they want and provide it before they even ask you for it.

Another roadblock for someone in my situation was licensing. To sell financial instruments, you needed to pass a series of exams that must be sponsored by your employer. While working in a middle office function, it was complicated to get sign-off for said sponsorship. For starters, it was costly. Secondly, it would likely increase turnover. Meanwhile, to qualify for a front office function, employers would ask if you were licensed. It's like that meme about an ad looking for a 'junior analyst' with five years of experience.

I felt trapped within the system. I applied to dozens of roles internally to no avail. I started to think about Ervo; maybe I needed to leave the industry altogether. There was one instance when I got a hiring manager to the point where she said she'd like to move forward. Then I had a conversation with my boss about potential next steps. When I got back to my desk there was a voicemail from the hiring manager saying she could no longer move forward. I had to go back my boss to tell him that I wasn't going anywhere. Talk about awkward conversations.

A year later, in 2015, I made the decision to exert all my efforts and earn a front office seat. I stumbled on an internal opening in a different area of the bank. The hiring manager was convinced that I could take on the role and said I'd have to pass the licensing exams within sixty days. I jumped on it immediately without giving much consideration to anything else about the role. It is extremely rare to find an opening where management will take a shot on you, so I had no choice but to accept. It was a front office sales role in a new part of the business. I thought it was an enticing challenge, so I took the leap and left my middle office function on excellent terms. Management understood that I was looking for an opportunity to expand my skillset and knowledge base.

I was on an emotional rollercoaster that entire year. I resented the bank for not going against the grain and continuing to foster an environment that, in my opinion, stunted career development. I was personally exhausted from interviews and rejections. Yet again, I found myself having to prove that I belonged somewhere. I struggled with it because I thought I'd reached a point in life where I could finally put that chip behind me.

My mind drew parallels between my desire to progress to the front office at JP Morgan and my brief teenage employment at McDonald's. Being trapped behind those terminals reminded me of sweaty afternoons flipping burgers over a piping hot grill in the back kitchen. In both cases, I was fighting to be front and center, because it's where I felt I belonged.

After accepting a front office seat, I reflected and acknowledged that this was another obstacle. As hard as it was, I wasn't going to be defined by my title. I was dared internally to prove them wrong.

✳

I transitioned to my new sales role in February, and the adjustment period proved to be manageable. I felt more in my element. The job was a stark contrast to my original entry into the bank; that first year where I felt like a deer in headlights. I was confident I'd pass my licensing exams, that I'd pick up a good understanding of the products, and that, eventually, I'd be impactful in my contributions to the team and the broader organization. Once I made it into the front office, there was a new pep in my step. I felt accomplished. Also, I was comforted by the absence of stress that came from finding a more suitable role.

Shortly after getting settled into the role, I began to think about my next personal undertaking. I spent the last four years exerting the majority of my effort towards my career. I battled through the hours at COMD; I knocked down the door at JP Morgan; and I finished up my MBA in the midst of all that. Lastly, I had tackled the uphill climb to the front office. I needed a break from work; I had to think about something else. I had to do something for me. I yearned to be more than my resume.

The weather was warming up. Maybe this would be an excellent opportunity to channel the lessons from that summer spent with Riad back in college. A physical challenge was what I needed. I wasn't in bad shape on paper, but I wasn't healthy either. My endurance levels were low; I hadn't lifted weights in years. I wasn't sure where to start; doubt crept in. Perhaps I wouldn't be able to commit to any training plans. I was so far removed from the last time I took fitness seriously that I wasn't sure I'd be successful.

At the time, I'd been living with a roommate and good friend, Farrell. It was coincidental that we ended up living together. I had met him back in high school at the same party that I met Kenny; the two of them were best friends since childhood. When I started to explore living in Manhattan, Kenny mentioned that Farrell was also looking to make a move, so we decided to give it a go. At this point, we were coming on five years together, and—for guys that had commitment issues with the ladies—we were pretty functional as roommates. We had different routines, so we complemented each other well. Farrell was usually up at the crack of dawn tackling a morning run or getting in a workout. In the evening, we'd come home at different times. I'd usually squeeze in a trip to the gym in our building. For the most part during the week, we'd be out of each other's way. On the weekend, we shared a circle of friends.

Farrell's discipline always intrigued me. He was systematic every morning. He'd admit that he doesn't sleep well generally, and that helps get him out of bed. But, from my point of view, I was envious of his routine. Also, he was a runner his entire life. He made the miles, and the pace looked easy. Meanwhile, I wasn't sure if I could even run a full mile.

I decided to join him for a run to learn a thing or two. I wanted to size up where I stood in comparison, though I was nervous to know the truth. To that point in my life, I'd never run more than three miles, and, usually, it was at a leisurely pace. Every now and then, I'd push myself, then slow down to catch my breath.

During our run, I found myself struggling to keep up. I'd never learned how to pace myself, so I'd sprint a short distance, stop to take a breath, and run some more. We were barely a half-mile in when Farrell stopped. He looked confused, then his face turned serious, as if he was about to break some bad news to me. I wasn't sure what he was going to say, but I knew that I was ruining the experience for him.

As it turned out, he softly pointed out that I was going about it wrong. Farrell proceeded to give me a piece of advice that has stuck with me forever since then. In fact, the wisdom of it transcends running.

"Look," he said, "I'm not sure what you're doing with all of the stop-and-go out here, but I've been doing this my whole life. The cardinal rule, when it comes to running long distances, is you can slow down as much as you like—I don't care if you're barely running at all—but, whatever you do, you cannot stop."

For a moment, I felt defensive.

"Who cares if I stop," I thought to myself. "I'm still getting a workout in. That's all that matters anyway. Maybe real runners don't stop, but I'm just here for the sweat."

Over the next few days I ran alone. I didn't want to be a burden to Farrell, slowing down his runs. But I kept thinking about his advice. The reason I agreed to run with him in the first place was that I wanted to learn the mindset behind his discipline. He ran long distances, and there was a parallel between that and searching for a purpose that stuck with me. I couldn't fully articulate it at the time, but, from that point forward, I never stopped mid-run again.

I was always a big believer in surrounding yourself with people who are better than you at different things. It takes humility, but the impact can be everlasting. Yet, it had been a while since I'd applied that belief. During that run with Farrell, my mindset started to shift. Slowly I found myself yearning to be empowered in this new area of my life. I was fortunate that one of my first 'teammates' was sharing an apartment with me the whole time.

**In the Words of Drake: "My Team Good"**

# 16

# Swerve

After taking Farrell's message deeply to heart, I felt like I was on to something. I acknowledged that I didn't have all the answers. What if I could find a group of people with 'Farrell-like' influence to surround me? Beyond running, what if I surrounded myself with folks who could push me to succeed in other endeavors, whether athletic or in other areas? In a city like New York, I was never going to succeed on my own, or at the very least it would prove to be exponentially more difficult.

When you think about 'team' as it pertains to a personal journey, it's fair to assume that family and close friends are the people you'd consult with before making decisions. I was thinking beyond that. I wanted to dig into the community. Knowing that the biggest grinders in the world live in my city, I desired to learn from them, and, eventually, be like them.

Before getting ahead of myself, I decided to focus on one goal; I wanted to devote myself to running. I wanted to prove to myself that I could commit, that I had what it takes to apply discipline.

Most importantly, I wanted to prove that, no matter how frustrating it might get, I wouldn't quit. I was consistently running on my own and over a month or two, I began to understand that my emphasis should not be on speed, but rather to build up my endurance. I had to take baby steps. I'd run a half-mile a few times a week, then the next week I'd increase it to three-quarters of a mile; the week after that I'd finally hit the mile mark. I kept reminding myself that I was physically out of shape, but that my mindset needed a re-tuning to sync with my body. I had to accomplish small wins to realize that I was capable of reaching a bigger goal.

That summer provided many moments of reflection. I started to rediscover elements of my childhood. Every time I hit a milestone, it reminded me of my younger battles; it reassured me that I was capable, but I had to keep pushing to redefine my physical limits. Aspects of that new definition included; running distances above five miles, and waking up in the darkness of winter to don layers of clothing and face the howling wind. Perhaps, one day, my new self would even sign up for a race and compete.

For the next year, I stuck to running. I started to play with my diet to figure out how to best take care of my body. I enjoyed the results I was seeing, but along the way I realized I was limiting myself to focus just on running. I hit a wall. I wasn't seeing any improved performance, and I wasn't sure why.

That period coincided with the rise of the boutique fitness era. Working at JP Morgan, I'd see companies like Lululemon on CNBC every day talking about exponential growth forecasts for the industry. The rise caught major cities like New York by storm; studios were popping up all over Manhattan. Social media feeds were flooded with folks sharing their favorite studios and workouts. I wanted to get in on the fun.

It just so happened, at that time, that some friends of mine from high school collaborated on a venture to open a spin studio called Swerve Fitness. Swerve was unique relative to their competition because they were more than just a cycling class with good music, they created a first of its kind 'team-based' experience.

Within the classes, teams of strangers rode together to collect points by spinning to a rhythm or by winning speed–based races. It was competitive and engaging at the same time. Although I had never spun before, I was intrigued by the concept.

I admired the founders who leaped (or rather "swerved") from their corporate jobs in finance to pursue an idea that, quite frankly, could have flopped in an unforgiving city. Opening any business in New York involves a multitude of hurdles. Owners must be prudent when beginning a company that's still in a 'proof of concept' phase as that is essentially 'going all in.'

I attended the launch and began taking classes regularly. At first, I was getting used to sitting on the bike and working with the gears. It took me several rides to find my sweet spot. But, in that period, I was getting hooked. I enjoyed everything from the competitions to the high-fiving of people who I'd just met to the positive messages shared by the community.

Somehow, Swerve fostered a competitive environment that left all egos outside the room. You could be an athlete your entire life, or you someone who committed to a fitness regime that week. In the darkness of the studio, there was no distinction. Regardless of your athletic background, everyone in the studio was there to be better than their last ride. At that point, it was everything I needed: a community of people who wanted to improve every day.

I called them my TEAM, and many of them were complete strangers. Teammates beside me in a dark room on a bike at 6 AM in the morning with an instructor in front pushing all of us to push ourselves. I was blindly pushing with no idea where I was going, grinding it out in New York City, focused on building my career, but also determined to be the best version of myself.

"Why do I rise at 4:30 AM to catch a cold subway car to get to class?" I wondered. "Why do these people, who I don't really know, mean so much to me?" Ultimately, I think my TEAM inspired me,; they helped me unleashed a potential which I'd never tapped.

It was in that dark room where personal reflection transcended the scoreboard, where I learned a phrase, often repeated by our lead instructor Dyan, "I Can, I Am, I Will."

＊

Swerve cultivated a community of empowerment and goal setting. One of the keys to their execution was that it never felt like a cult. We were a group of people figuring it out together, and that was comforting. The community encouraged you to commit to yourself to any ambition, whether it was athletic, professional, or personal. And they pushed you to follow through. The focus was to bring out the best in each other by working together. That was the allure as far as I was concerned.

The Swerve class model was metric–based, but metrics couldn't be steered by one individual. It had to be a team of people working together, so as the brand developed, the concept went beyond the studio. Several times I found myself talking to someone I just met, thinking, "This person somehow pushed me to a new goal inside the studio, I wonder what they could do if I brought them into my life out here."

It was the winter of 2014. I was balanced between running and Swerve. I felt my endurance building, and my confidence as an athlete growing. I channeled energy from my newfound discipline and from those on my TEAM. I had musings around what this new energy meant, what exactly I could do with it. I'd surrounded myself with college athletes, marathon runners, and triathletes. Somehow, I kept up with them.

"Is it possible that maybe it's not too late for me to do something that I once thought too grand for me?" I thought.

I had no idea what the ceiling of my abilities was. Maybe I was getting ahead of myself. It's just that I was so damn motivated by the people around me.

As the new year rolled around, I put reservations aside; I signed up for a half marathon. It was my first significant race; in fact, it was the first time I ever paid to run. The race would be later in the year. I had plenty of time to prepare, but that didn't erase my fears or doubts. Negative thoughts immediately invaded my mind.

"I'm not a real runner; I just like to run for exercise. Thirteen miles is crazy! I'm a five-mile guy at max. I peaked athletically in the spin studio; I should be proud of that. If I do finish this race successfully, does that mean I have to run more?"

In the fitness industry, the busiest time of year is January, when everyone makes their annual New Years resolutions. Swerve was no different. The studio saw an influx of people. They had a board near the front desk where they encouraged everyone to write down a personal goal on a Post-It note. A couple of months before the race, I wrote, "Complete a half marathon."

Every time I'd walk into the studio, I saw that bright yellow square staring me down. It undoubtedly kept me accountable as I trained. Not only did I have to see every week, but then I had to engage with TEAM. They knew the truth; they had seen my goal, too. And, remember, those were very people who were pushing me to push myself.

Training for the half marathon never got manageable, but the more I built up my mileage, the more I began to believe I'd cross the finish line. Up to race day, the most I had ever run was eleven miles. Most books on training suggest that you not push it to thirteen in order to avoid the chance of injury.

September came quickly. On the day of race the weather was perfect. It was being held in the Hamptons, and, while I felt ready physically, I had one obstacle to overcome that day: my mindset. I had to remind myself that I was about to do something I'd never done before. I had to cross a finish line. It was me versus myself, and sometimes that's the beauty of running.

Before race day, I'd connected with my friend, Eric, one of the Swerve co-founders. I asked him if he had any apparel I could wear for the race. Swerve was so critical to me accomplishing my goal that I wanted to represent them any way I could. He gave me a bright green tank top. When I put it I realized that I should have thrown in a few push-ups while training. But, it didn't matter; I was proud to have a part of Swerve with me for the half marathon.

Since this was my first race, I had no routine. I ate a banana that morning, drank lots of water, and reminded myself to *breathe*. At the start line, my palms began to sweat. I forced my eyes shut and focused on being in the moment. The gun went off. I was cruising, breathing in through the nose and out through the mouth. I always loved the Hamptons in the summertime; I took in everything, from the smell of the beach air to the grandeur of the real estate.

At the ten–mile marker, I started to lose momentum. This was near my maximum distance; I was embarking on new territory. Inwardly I repeated Dyan's message, "I Can, I Am, I Will." I pushed through those last three miles. Before I knew it, a volunteer placed a medal over my head. I'd never experienced that before, certainly not for an athletic accomplishment. I felt unworthy because I knew I didn't accomplish this on my own. Heck, if I'd never met Dyan I don't know how I would've completed the race.

My parents were at the finish line. It was the first time they'd ever seen a race in person; it was all so new to them. It wasn't like watching a basketball game where they could follow a scoreboard or congratulate me on my stat sheet. They were proud of me for achieving a goal I'd set for myself, but they had no idea how to quantify the accomplishment. They had no understanding of what it meant to finish a race. But, then, neither did I.

I wasn't sure about what would happen next. My parents and I went out to lunch to celebrate. Over the coming weeks, I went back to my routine at Swerve. In those early morning rides, alone with my thoughts, I reflected on answering that question.

"What's next?"

# Kitchen Table

After finishing that first race in the Hamptons, I had a feeling of emptiness. I think this is the case anytime there is an extended build-up to an event. I'd spent nearly six months focusing on the half marathon. Once it was over, there wasn't immediately anything available to replace it.

I didn't want to take a step back from running. I'd put in the time to get myself in shape; I feared what would happen if I slowed down. Would sustain my form? On the other hand, I wasn't really a victim of the racing bug; I wasn't rushing to sign up for my next competition. I wanted to be thoughtful about my next step.

My choice was made for me a week later; I received an email from one of my more prominent clients. It was an invitation to run a half marathon in Denver, just six weeks away. I didn't hesitate (not that I had much choice) and I signed up immediately. It felt right. I was happy knowing that I still had more miles ahead of me. It was good to know that I wasn't settling back into whatever my 'normal' routine had been before the half marathon in the Hamptons.

In the days after, I realized that I hadn't considered one factor: I had never run in the elements. This was going to be at the end of October, in the 'mile-high' city of Denver. I was nervous. I had no idea what I'd be up against, so I ran extra miles while training in an attempt to compensate for the unknown.

The weekend of the half marathon came around; I arrived in Denver three days ahead of time in order to acclimate, if only slightly, to the altitude. I made a point to go on a light run each day. On race day, the climate was cool and brisk; I had to put on an extra layer. This time around, I felt more prepared mentally. I was looking forward to Mile Ten because I wanted to stare it down, knowing I'd defeated it before.

The gun went off, and I hit my stride early on. I could tell that my prep–runs were paying off. The whole race felt good. As I crossed the finish line, the clock showed "1:45:08." At first, I didn't know what that meant, then I checked my pace. I'd run at nearly an eight-minute pace the entire race. That was the moment that the racing bug bit me. I knew I had more courses coming my way.

Over the next two years, I ran a dozen more races across the country—the majority of which I ran alone. Along the way, I shared my experiences with my TEAM at Swerve. I was proud that I didn't call it quits after that first race in the Hamptons. Yet, I still had no idea if there would come a point in time when I'd hang up the old running shoes. I noticed that there were many runners in the field in their forties, fifties, sixties, and beyond. I wasn't sure if, one day, that would be me.

Little did I know that, once I started to feel accomplished, my TEAM had other ideas in mind. They had begun to dip into the triathlon circuit, and invited me to level up and take on a new challenge. I couldn't resist. What drew me in was the reality that my TEAM was composed of ordinary people, not athletes. They didn't stick out, yet they were challenging themselves extraordinarily. It became evident that if I set my mind to it, I could do something extraordinary as well.

My TEAM, those strangers I'd met in a dark room, encouraged me to get comfortable with something that made me uneasy. Sure, I embraced running, but I wasn't a swimmer. I didn't enjoy it; I never felt confident in the water. I couldn't imagine myself competing against any sort of current.

I started out slow with a couple of sprint distance triathlons in Long Island and Westchester. The swim portion proved to be my biggest challenge, and it showed in the results. I did my best to make up for the lost time on the bike and the run portions. One thing was clear—no matter how much I hated the swim, I was going to keep showing up. Even so, the finishes were similar to the half marathon in the Hamptons, afterward there was always a small void inside myself.

I tested my limits mentally and physically, uncovering more potential with each race. I'd flashback to the days at Swerve, before I ever crossed a finish line, and think, "These are great experiences, but how do I build on this? What happens next?'

\*

I should've known that more was coming my way. Unbeknownst to me, my TEAM had their own thoughts; they decided it was time to up the ante. In December of 2016, I found myself signing up for a Half Ironman scheduled to take place just six months later: an event in Maryland called Eagleman.

"Okay, Bishoy," I thought, "You've outdone yourself. What the hell are you trying to prove? Just eighteen months ago, you couldn't run 13.1 miles. Now, like a maniac, you signed up to compete in a 70.3–mile race."

A Half Ironman starts in the water with a 1.2–mile swim; you follow that with a 56–mile bike ride; then bring it all home with a 13.1–mile run. And that's 'half;' imagine doing a 'full' Ironman. I was scared shitless of what I had agreed to, yet I felt compelled to hide my fear. I didn't want anyone seeing my vulnerability.

For the next five months of training, I decided to isolate myself. I wanted to give my body and mind the best shot at preparing for what I knew would be a daunting experience.

People around me asked, "Bishoy, why are you doing this?"

I had no answer. In fact, I put my social life on hold. Instead, I watched my diet and steered clear of alcohol during my training period. My mother was concerned that I was putting all my energy toward the Half Ironman, and none toward my dating life.

I questioned myself as well, but then I'd think of my TEAM. I knew that—although I had no immediate response—backing out was not an option. My heart told me that there's a purpose behind this, so I pushed forward blindly. I kept on with my routine.

I noticed my body transforming during the five months, but at no point could I confidently say I felt ready. I had no idea what Ironman shape was. I wasn't going to know until race day. I wanted to hedge my bets; I started looking around for a less intense race after Eagleman to sign up for. In case something went wrong, I'd be able to make up for it by competing elsewhere.

I had my eye on the New York City Marathon. Even though, I'd never ran more than fifteen miles, I felt that my body could take on the immense challenge of twenty-six. And, best of all, there was no swimming. I thought about it seriously, but didn't pull the trigger.

It wasn't long after that I went home for a Saturday brunch with my family. It was always tough to make our plans sync up, and I was looking forward to my mother's cooking. That particular day, she prepared a spread. We were catching up around the kitchen table, filling each other in on our lives. Usually, this meant my mom grilling Vina and me about our careers, and our love lives. To her dismay, we wouldn't have much to update her on.

One good thing about all of the races that I'd been completing was that it provided me ammo for switching topics. I decided to tell my parents that I was thinking about signing up for the New York City Marathon in November. My mother looked rattled.

"Why? How?" she said with concern.

I tried explaining to her that the New York City Marathon was a spectacle. Even though a Half Ironman was a feat of endurance, the New York City Marathon was going to be more meaningful to me one day when I looked back.

She looked at my father, perhaps waiting for his disapproval. Then she looked back at me with disappointment. It was only a second before she spoke, but it felt like an eternity.

"Your father and I have booked a trip to Israel in November. So, unfortunately, we're going miss you running in the Marathon."

I breathed a sigh of relief. That explained the look in her eyes.

"In any case," she continued, "I'm more concerned about this seventy-mile race you signed up for. We won't miss that one. And, if you can finish that, I'm not worried about twenty-six miles."

I guess my mother's rationale made sense. I hadn't completed either competition at that point, but she was right; if I could do the Eagleman, I could do the New York City Marathon. And, as far as their trip to Israel, I thought to myself, "I'm an adult. I don't need mom and dad at every race. I'll send them pictures."

# Mile 40

June was quickly approaching and, even though I'd started planting seeds for the TCS NYC Marathon later in the year, I knew I still had an enormous task ahead of me: Eagleman. I checked the weather for days leading up to the race; at the very least, I needed the forecast to be on my side.

The truth of the matter is that race day is the simple part. The hard part is those months of training: months of working out twice a day, of forcing yourself to get up early and run in bad weather, of jumping in a cold pool to shock your body. It also includes trying new diets in the hopes that one syncs with your training regimen, and telling your friends that you're busy on weekends.

You can consult all the pros and read all the books but, at the end of the day, you are one that has to look in the mirror. You are the one who has to commit and accept that it's going to hurt. You have to know that you might stumble and fall along the way but, ultimately, you will be better for it.

I reflected on those five months. I acknowledged the work I did. Parts of the process were unmistakably dark and lonely. On several occasions, driven by self-doubt, I wanted to quit. But looking back, I didn't have a single regret. In the days leading up to the race, I was at ease knowing I gave it my all to get myself to that start line.

As the weekend rolled around, I arrived in Maryland. The forecast predicted 93 degrees Fahrenheit on race day. The night before, I prepped peanut butter and banana sandwiches; I laid out all of my gear; and I set my alarm for the morning. I felt the adrenaline kicking in. I knew I wasn't going to get much sleep, but I was so zoned in that I didn't care.

Early next morning, as the sun crept into my room, I was awake before the alarm clock went off. I jumped in the shower. Then, after toweling off, I stared at myself in the mirror. I reassured myself that, by the end of the day, I'd be able to say I did something crazy.

Soon thereafter I was at the event. I went to the transition area to set up my towels, bike gear, and running shoes. Then I walked around the area, sizing up the competitors. The fascinating thing about triathletes is that most of them look like regular folks. Even at an Ironman, much of the field blended in. That fact is reassuring but also nerve-wracking when you consider how deceptively quick some of them are. I put that out of my mind to focus on positive thoughts. There was no room for anything else on a day like this.

I paced over to the start, closed my eyes, and gave myself a nod of confidence. The race was about to kick off.

"If I just make it through the swim portion, then the rest of the race will take care of itself," I assured myself.

I had two rules for the swim: 1) You can slow down, but don't stop (similar to Farrell's guidance on running); and 2) No matter what, do not look back. If you stop, you'll lose momentum. If you look back, you'll realize how far you are from shore.

I dove into the water and swam to the side to avoid the scrum in the middle. I repeated the two rules over and over again, to remind myself. It helped to stop my mind from wandering.

"Don't stop. Don't look back."

I didn't pay attention to the competition; I didn't want anything to distract me. I had one goal in the water: to simply to get back on land. After an hour of paddling, I made it out. My legs were wobbly; my heart was beating fast. I required some assistance to remove my wetsuit. Then I looked up at the summer sky, smiled, and let out a huge sigh of relief.

I had finished the hardest swim of my life. Even better, I did it in a reasonable time. But I didn't have a moment to celebrate, I had to transition to the bike portion of the race.

In preparation, I had spent countless hours in the cycling studio. I wasn't solely accumulating mileage, I consistently outperformed everyone else in my classes. I was always at the top of the pack. In the weeks before the race, I rode outside. This proved to be more trying on my body as a result of the rugged terrain which amplified my soreness afterward. That said, I completed the longer distances in good time, and I felt that I was well conditioned by race day. Of all three parts of an Ironman, biking was my strong suit.

*

The day before the race I inspected the bike I'd ordered from a New York–based bike shop. Due to some travel logistics that week, I had to make the arrangements in a rush. To my dismay, I'd been sent a hybrid instead of a road bike.

I couldn't afford to panic; I had to roll with the punches. I called the bike shop to inquire about the mix-up. They admitted that they had erred as a result of a significant bike tour the same weekend as Eagleman—I wouldn't be charged. The man on the phone asked me what I was using the bike for. I said, "Eagleman." In a sarcastic tone, he wished me "good luck."

Now, as I transitioned from the swim to my bike, those two words and his biting tone rushed into my head. I couldn't help but think the worst. Yes, I was relieved to be out of the water, but there was no way the remaining sixty-nine miles would go smoothly.

I put on my socks and running shoes. I adjusted the seat. Then I quietly followed the other bikes out of the transition area, anxious to see how my hybrid would hold up.

The first ten miles, I was peddling harder than usual. But, since I was surrounded by other riders, I figured I was fine. Another five miles went by. Suddenly, the cyclist beside me had a tire burst. He wobbled to the side of the road. More out of instinct than conscious thought, I pulled over to help.

The truth is I'm not very mechanical. I had no idea what to do besides keep him company. But he wasn't in search of moral support; he wanted a technician. I was not his man. I got back on my much-too-heavy hybrid, and took a deep breath. I was only fifteen miles in, but it felt as though I'd exerted enough energy to have traveled twice that distance. Looking at my watch, I realized that I was off my target time. I wasn't holding myself accountable to a strict pace, but I wanted to stay consistent with my training. I asked the cyclist once more if he was going to be okay. He gave me the green light, and I took off again.

I rode another five miles. It felt like I was peddling in quicksand. I was barely a third of the way in, summoning all of my will power to keep focused on the road ahead. Other bikes were cruising by, their riders screaming "On your left" to announce their presence. I was chugging along, looking for the next significant mile marker, looking for a sign to tell me that I'm one step closer to the end. The farther I rode, the more isolated I felt. Bikes glided past me. I was giving it my all, but it felt like I was stuck in one place.

To give you an idea of the difference between a hybrid and a road bike, imagine taking a vacation in a tropical climate. You made plans to rent a car, perhaps a nice, high-speed premium convertible. But, instead of that, you receive a beat-up minivan with a broken air conditioner. That's what it felt like slogging along under the sun in Maryland, like I was stuck with a clunker.

It was 10 AM; I was on pace to finish the bike portion of the race well behind my desired time. I'd be transitioning at the next station around noon. That meant I'd begin my run at the hottest point of the day. I had made it to the midway point of the bike ride. I was thirsty, but I was stubborn; I didn't want to stop. I was determined to push myself to the next marker.

An eternity went by. Finally, I saw a sign for Mile 36.

"Why didn't I stop at the last water station?" I asked myself. "There's not going to be another one for while, and it's only getting hotter. You're an idiot, Bishoy."

I still had twenty miles to go. That's the equivalent of one Swerve class. I knew I could make it. My breathing became more labored, but my mind stayed focused on the road ahead.

At Mile 40, my legs felt like two chunks of lead. If I was a car, my gas tank's 'empty' light would have lit up. My entire body was riding on fumes. My eyes searched the road for a metaphorical gas station. But there was no relief in sight.

At Mile 40, my legs came to a halt.

I stopped completely. The thing I said I'd never do.

I looked around. The road was empty, not a single rider in sight. I was alone in a hot asphalt desert. I looked down at my arms. They were covered in salt from dehydration. I wiped my head: more salt.

The nearest hydration station was ten miles away, but I was exhausted. I wasn't sure how I'd manage to get there. My thoughts grew increasingly dark.

"Is it time to quit?" I wondered. "Do I really belong out here? My parents are waiting at the finish line. Maybe I should phone my mom. I could just call it a day. Get out of this mess."

Suddenly, I remembered I was about to turn thirty. I had chosen this path. Now I imagined calling my mother to bail me out.

I was at rock bottom, physically and mentally.

Finally it made sense to me why, for the last five months, people kept asking, "Why are you doing this?" At that dark moment, I was asking the very same question. But I had no answer. I felt doomed. I was a failure—an embarrassment to myself, to my parents, and to my TEAM. My thoughts spiraled tirelessly into the void.

I found myself feverishly thinking about other moments in life where I felt as defeated, every other Mile 40. I did it to summon a familiar response, and to calibrate those previous experiences against this one. In doing so, I made a turning point realization.

I had been in tough situations before but, in this case, the problem was self-induced. I had signed up, paid for the event, and prepared to get to Mile 40. No one else had placed me here. It was on me to get to that finish line. Under that hot sun, miles away from water, I had collect my thoughts in order to arrive at Mile 70. I forced myself to dig deeper than ever before. I repeated the phrase, "I Can, I Am, I Will." No matter what it took, I was going to finish.

I still had doubts. My mind and heart were in a confrontation with each other. My mind said, "You're gassed. There's nothing you can do at this point. Call it a day." Yet my heart stepped in to remind me that I had always found the inner strength for every other battle. Despite the obstacles, I could break barriers.

Somehow, I made it to the hydration station. Do you remember those old Gatorade commercials? The ones where the energy drink seemed to flow through a person's pores? That's precisely what I looked like. I must've chugged gallons. I reeked of yellow Gatorade for the rest of the race, but at least I finished the bike portion.

Once I made it to the run station, I realized the conditions were dire. I broke down the distance remaining. Thirteen was too big a number. To make my goal manageable, I'd need to run one mile at a time. I was ready to crawl if I had to, inch by inch. I wasn't going to let my TEAM down.

On the outside, I probably looked defeated, like I could collapse at any moment. It wasn't pretty. Yet, on the inside, I knew that I was going to finish. Farrell's voice rang in my head. Even though I was running at a snail's pace, I wasn't going to stop.

Nearly eight hours after I started that morning, I crossed the finish line. My mind came to a crashing halt. I turned around and saw the video screen of finishers.

"What the hell did I do?" I thought. "*Why* the hell did I do it?"

People hugged me and congratulated me. My mother had a look like I had come out of surgery with a favorable prognosis. I didn't have much to say, but I was smiling, happy to be done for the day. In the midst of all the excitement, I reflected that my mantra of breaking barriers was no longer a theory; it was a proven concept.

I believe that obstacles are put in front of you to dare you—like I was alone at Mile 40—and never to define you. That's why I was compelled to push onward after I hit rock bottom. It was a sense of duty. Now I knew it was my time to pay it forward. I'd been holding onto something for so long, a magic formula for success. I needed to tell someone, anyone that would listen.

# Break Barriers

# 19

# A Flame Ignited

On the car ride home from Maryland, my parents talked about how they had been impressed by the vast field of competitors. There were several participants in their own age bracket, and they praised them for their commitment to training; they expressed that they wouldn't even know where to begin.

Meanwhile, I was in the back seat with my friend Skyler. He was no rookie to these courses; his father was a triathlete, and he coached me through in the months of training. I was reeling off the high of finishing, that I powered through in a moment of despair. I was talking to him about how I wanted my next dose; I spoke of one day completing a full Ironman; I spoke about doing multiple competitions a year. I felt no bounds to what I could take on.

My mom peeked around from the passenger's seat like an alarm just buzzed off in her head from overhearing me. She sighed at the realization that I made it through the weekend in one piece, but she was also hoping that perhaps I had my fill, that maybe I wouldn't want to re-live Mile 40.

I made it back to New York that evening. I showered, got a haircut, and took myself out to a hearty dinner to acknowledge my finish, I figured I had some calories to spare. As I was eating, I recalled the agreement I made with myself that barring no significant injury or letdown at Eagleman, I was going to knock off a bucket list item and run the TCS New York City Marathon in November of that year. If I felt energized enough to tell Skyler I would compete in multiple Ironman races on the ride home then I could run a marathon.

My thoughts were brewing around my finish line moment, I toyed with the idea of using the TCS NYC Marathon as my platform to share my story, to let the world know how unstoppable I felt and to hopefully give hope to someone who was seeking it. At that moment, I felt that something big was going to happen for me and I couldn't explain it, the universe had me feeling I was on the verge of something, but I kept suppressing it fearful that my emotions were still running high after the race.

I decided to move forward with that plan to register for the TCS New York City Marathon. To gain entry to the race, you must either get in through a drawing or raise money for charity. The former is not easy, with over 50,000 participants vying for a spot. I had to consider if I wanted to fundraise and if so, I had to decide which charity I should fundraise for.

This was happening I thought, I can use my personal story for a good cause; many of my peers were unaware of my background, and it would catch them off guard, propelling the story's impact.

At the same time, I thought about the positive impact I might have. I also struggled mightily, and I pushed back on myself, thinking, "What if people don't care? What if I put myself out there and no one donates?"

I was at a point in my life where I was uncovering my potential on various fronts, but by all means I was still vulnerable. I didn't want to expose my weaknesses, and I ultimately didn't want to fail or embarrass myself. So, I then decided to write out my story, and for a few days I put it aside. I was keen on sharing a message of hope focused more on my mindset of breaking barriers as opposed to just sharing a biographical timeline of my bout with leukemia.

I titled it *The Comeback is Always Greater Than the Setback*, and the words flowed. It was as if I wanted to write the piece for years and had held it in. It was extremely therapeutic, and I started to look for pictures to depict my journey. I called my mom and told her to dig up old photos. She was a little reluctant, perhaps because that task took her back to those dark days. I smiled when she gave me the collection, and I saw a picture of the child who lost his hair because of chemo side-by-side with an image of the man touting his Ironman medal.

I thought it was fair to assume that everyone would likely agree with the sentiment that cancer is evil, and that we should support efforts to eradicate it. However, I wasn't in a position to drive a scientific result personally. I thought, if anything, I was more likely to impact others by giving hope, by letting them know that, through cancer, I found a strength that carried me through nearly thirty years of ups and downs.

I wanted to focus less on iterating a story that folks were already familiar with. There are thousands of people who fundraise each year, and I was focused on my desire to deliver a personal message. That message derived from the fact that cancer gave me a bad hand earlier in life, and I wanted to share a mindset that encouraged others to tackle the hands they've been dealt using the tenors that helped me.

I didn't care if I was helping someone in the hospital going through treatment, or if it was helping a family member who was coping with the diagnosis, or even if it merely touched someone who was going through a rough patch outside of the medical arena. For me, the tenors applied in all areas of my life; they went beyond cancer.

I was passionate in my drive to help people realize that barriers are meant to be broken, that they will make it if they abide by patience, perspective, and purpose. I didn't have ties to any relevant charities directly, and so I looked for an organization that linked most closely with my story. I chose the Leukemia and Lymphoma Society.

I had not known much about the organization or its programs. However, my research into their footprint made me comfortable with the decision to work with them. The fundraising minimum was $3,000 for race entry, and I was committed. I deliberated if I should pay the minimum out-of-pocket—feeling satisfied that I supported a relevant charity—and shift gears to focus on training for the actual race.

I tackled the idea for days, struggling to make a decision. I thought about the fact that I don't like asking people for money and the thought of fundraising made me a little uncomfortable. I also considered my parents and my sister, and how perhaps this might affect them. This was not just my story; it was our story. Were they ready to be reminded of those difficult times? I knew I couldn't half-ass it. If I was doing this, I was putting all my cards on the table. I needed guidance in making a decision, I wasn't sure where to go. I was seeking a third party, someone who wasn't personally tied to the story.

During the spring of that year, as I was training for Eagleman, I started exploring new opportunities for promotional roles at JP Morgan. I needed a new challenge, I felt as though I had proven myself as a talented salesperson, and management had begun to take note as I was awarded for my work.

I recall there was one opening that I had applied for and it was a couple of weeks into the hiring process at that point. I approached the hiring manager's assistant Gloria, and I had asked her if she could squeeze me in for fifteen minutes on his calendar. In spite of his tight travel schedule, she was kind enough to help me out, and she arranged for our meeting. I tailored my resume, and I looked forward to presenting myself as a candidate that he never saw coming. I felt like I had nothing to lose; I knew I could do the job if given the opportunity. But I also knew I was up against the clock; he already met with several qualified candidates.

A week later, the time for our meeting came around. I sat down in his office and Tim, the hiring manager, cheerfully asked me how he could help me and what it is I wanted to talk to him about. Before a word came out of my mouth, I found solace in his tone, his stature as he leaned in, and his bright smile. I thought to myself, "This is a guy who isn't afraid to shake things up. He's loud and awfully energetic, looking to light up the room at any cost."

I took a quick breath and said, "Thanks for taking the time to meet me, Tim. I'm here to tell you why I think I'm a good candidate for your opening."

He looked at me directly, and I could tell that he was listening to what I had to say. My boldness did not phase him. He wasn't looking for someone to suck up to him; he was looking for someone to impress him.

He struck a chord with me right away because it was in that meeting that I realized he was unique. He was the type of leader that sought to capitalize on your strengths and bring out the best in you. He was not intimidating or overbearing; he was personable. He cared about what I was saying, even when I wasn't sure if I should be saying it.

As I suspected then, he was very far along in the hiring process, and he made the decision to move forward with a great candidate. It appeared I did something right, however, because he followed up with me and he insisted I make every effort to stay in front of him —not the usual reaction from hiring managers that pass on you. Sometimes they say it, but he was pressing, and I felt wanted. He showed a genuine interest in my career development, and his ability to engage made me yearn for his mentorship. So I made it a point to catch up with him for breakfast or lunch every time he was in New York. I would update him on my progress professionally.

In July of 2017, as I was thinking about fundraising, and I was looking for that third party, I decided to share my story with him and see what he had to say. I hadn't really ever discussed my personal life with him. However, my gut told me that he is someone I could be vulnerable in front of. I trusted his leadership as a proven salesperson, and I would feel reassured if he saw potential in the message I was trying to put out there. I showed him the write-up that I was sitting on. He read it, smiled, and said, "You need to make that goal a little higher." Then he proceeded to make a generous donation.

He got serious, and told me that I need to aim high always. He wanted me to make my goal $100,000 while I only had it listed at $3,000. I got all bashful and said, "I don't know, Tim. That sounds a little ambitious." He said sternly, "Trust me. You must raise this goal." So I agreed to meet in the middle, and make it $50,000.

I was nervous. My heart started to beat quickly; I knew that Tim was right. He ignited a mighty flame. I had been building my story throughout a lifetime and, for the last few years, I was uncovering my capabilities at each race I signed up for, and every finish line I crossed.

I was looking for someone to push me to unleash the burden of holding onto this story, and I needed to feel that someone believed in me, and Tim was that person. If I had never interviewed for that role on his team, I never would have met him. It felt like destiny. The universe put us in front of each other, and that push he gave me meant more to me than any position.

It was in that room where he embodied the true meaning of mentor. Tim had absolutely nothing to gain from this, but he saw the potential. I immediately got to work comforted to know he was behind me.

*

Once I decided to fundraise, I found myself balancing an internal struggle. I wanted to ride Tim's wave of positivity. I also wanted to believe that my story was powerful enough to break a significant fundraising milestone, enough to be impactful. However, I didn't want to inundate people; I didn't want to be a burden.

During that first month of fundraising, things kicked off nicely, to my delight. I got a text message from two friends of mine, Rob and Will. They were business partners who run a hospitality group (NIEUW Group) managing bars and restaurants in New York and Washington D.C.

They had been acquaintances of mine through mutual friends who invested in their restaurants for several years. They saw a social media post that I had shared around my campaign, and they reached out to set up a lunch with me at their downtown location, Manhattan Proper.

I wasn't sure how we could possibly work together and what they might have in mind. I really respected both of them and their grit when it came to running their business, so I was excited to catch up with them.

We sat around the table, and I ordered my go-to item, the buffalo chicken sandwich. As the order was being prepared, Rob kicked off the conversation. "We see what you're doing," he said. "And we want in. Whatever you want from us, if you want our space or our sponsorship, tell us how we can help."

I fell back in my seat, slightly scratching my head to not look too surprised, thinking, "This is the start of something special."

I nodded and listened to all they had to say. I told them how appreciative I was of the fact that they approached me and I wanted them (and their brand) by my side every step of the way on the march to $50K. I barely finished my sandwich, chugged my water, shook their hands, and went home confident that my campaign just leveled up.

That meeting with Rob and Will meant the world to me, especially at a moment where it felt like maybe I was undertaking the campaign alone. I knew that they had my back; I was building an army of people looking to spread a positive message. That support meant more to me than the resources they had offered up, that was just the cherry on top.

On the way home I thought, "These are two excellent people, and there's a way we can all come out on top here. The onus is on me to commit to them the way they committed to me, especially when they didn't have to."

I hosted all of my relevant events exclusively at their venues, and I shouted them out at any opportunity I could. I wish I could do more. I feel forever indebted to them for taking the first step. They never asked me for anything and, when I needed their help with expenses for an event, they didn't blink before covering it. I was encouraged by them and their spirit. I wanted everyone in my campaign to know that their business was first class.

It was because of them that I started thinking strategically about other means to fundraise beyond personal donations. I realized that companies can benefit from getting behind a positive message, so I was emboldened to approach business owners to make the ask. Had they not believed in me, I would have left those opportunities untapped.

## 20

# Closing Bell

I have to admit that, initially, I was timid around publicly sharing my story. It's one thing to share it privately with family and friends; however taking that next step, it felt like once I put it out there, it was no longer mine. I was fully exposed.

I also realized that the longer I held out, the more significant a strain it might put on fundraising potential. So I eventually caved, and once my story was out there on social media, we began to conquer new milestones. First, we hit $15,000 and then $20,000 and, before I knew it, the race was six weeks away.

It was around then that the Leukemia and Lymphoma Society asked me if they could submit my story to the public relations team at New York Road Runners (the organization behind the TCS New York City Marathon). This team filters through stories to determine which ones will get featured coverage in the days leading up to, and during, the race's national telecast.

Since I had no expectations of any coverage, I joked around with friends when I got the note. I had always laughed and told them that one day I'd be found on the 'Sightings' section of Page Six of the New York Post, and perhaps this was my ticket. All kidding aside, I was happy knowing that donations continued to roll in.

October came around, and I got an email saying that New York Road Runners wanted to feature me in the 'Faces of the Marathon' Press Conference. I had no idea what it meant, but it sounded like a big deal. I immediately called my campaign manager to get an explanation. She said that only a handful of runners were selected. I needed to make myself available for media events, and prepare for a few shots for a commercial that would go live before the broadcast.

I had two immediate thoughts: one, I need to get a haircut; and two, this is going to be a massive boost for fundraising.

After gathering my thoughts, I took a screenshot of the email, and shared the update with my followers on social media. I was getting private messages in all directions congratulating me, and within hours, I was at nearly $30,000 in funds raised. After that day, I somehow found myself atop the Marathon's leaderboard of individual fundraisers for the Leukemia and Lymphoma Society.

That email was a trigger; the campaign immediately scaled up, and for the first time since Tim pushed me to get out there, I felt a responsibility. This marathon was no longer about me; it was about all of the people who believed in the message.

In those weeks I received support from people who connected to my story personally, people who I hadn't spoken to in years, or even people who I didn't even know kept up with my posts. I had to remind myself at times that I have an actual day job as well.

At one of my Saturday family brunches around the kitchen table, my mother encouraged me to be proud of the milestones we had already attained. With the best of intentions, she was trying to make sure I wouldn't be disappointed if we didn't get to $50,000. I realized she was right. Even if I am a dreamer, it would be a tall task nearly doubling the total funds raised in five weeks before the race. I refused to give up on the goal, but I was tempted to settle.

While shuffling a chaotic schedule between my day job, fundraising for the marathon, and hosting events to bolster awareness, I was conscientious to not ignore my friends. I didn't want to isolate myself. In fact, I needed them to maintain my sanity.

It was the middle of October, and on a Thursday night, when my friend Tony invited me out to Long Island City to hang out. He took me to his local bowling alley. He'd recently picked up the hobby, and so he was spending a lot of time there.

We walked in; everyone knew Tony's name. We played a couple of frames; I managed to keep up with him in the first frame. But he was only warming up; he crushed me on the next two. Afterward, Tony suggested we check out a local brewery that had just opened up. It was a work night, and I'm not much of a night owl, but I thought, "I never get to hang with my pal, Tony. Let's do it!"

As we got our first round, he finally asks me about my campaign. I didn't want to bring it up because I was pretty sure everyone had quite enough from my social media posts. He told me he respected what I was doing, and wanted to help out somehow. Tony had a vast network and close ties with various charitable organizations.

Just that week, one of the charities he worked with was invited by NASDAQ to ring the closing bell. He told me about the experience and how it boosted awareness for the organization.

"This week," Tony said, "I'm taking my contact at NASDAQ out to an event as a gesture of gratitude. Do you mind if I share your story? Who knows? They might take a bite at it."

I couldn't help but laugh.

"C'mon, Tony," I said, "Are you serious? I think that's highly unlikely. Even if they were interested, the marathon's just a few weeks away. There's no way they could arrange it that quickly."

"Go ahead," I continued, "I don't mind if you pass it along, but that I'm not holding my breath."

I thanked him for being so thoughtful; it meant a lot that he even offered it up. It was getting late, so we called it a night.

As the following week rolled around, I had almost forgotten about Tony's offer. I wasn't even sure if he had gone out with his contact yet, and I didn't bother following up. Then, all of a sudden, on Friday, October 27, I got an email from NASDAQ. The body read, "Closing Bell is a go."

I was talking to a client on the phone as I got that email and I immediately lost track of what I was saying. I couldn't believe what I was reading. I couldn't believe he made it happen.

I wrapped up the call with my client in a hurry and jumped into a conference room to tell my parents. They were about to take off for Israel the next day. I was talking so quickly they couldn't piece it together. But once I slowed down, and my parents realized what happened, they were simultaneously shocked and thrilled. I could sense in my dad's voice that his FOMO (Fear Of Missing Out, for you old timers) was kicking in. They deliberated if they should stay and I told them to go ahead with their trip.

NASDAQ sent over a flurry of emails with documents that I had to complete, and they notified me that I was going to be interviewed live around my campaign. I had asked them if Kenny and my friend Mark—who were also running the marathon for charitable causes that year—could join me. I thought it would be a cool experience for us to have together, and they approved it as a panel-style interview. A day afterward, I was going to be back in the studio as the featured guest, front and center at the Closing Bell ceremony on October 31.

It was surreal how quickly things escalated. One day I was firing out donation request emails and running out of ideas for social media posts, and the next day I am filling out information for a press release. I encountered a quick moment of panic because although my campaign took off, I wasn't talking about it much at work. I didn't think it was appropriate to solicit donations from co-workers, and I wanted to fly under the radar as much as possible in the office. The problem with this platform, in particular, is that when you work in a bank there are TVs everywhere and they are all set to CNBC, which features the bell ceremony daily. On October 31, I left work early trying to be sly without telling most of the people around me my plans.

NASDAQ's studio was right in the heart of Times Square, which I generally like to avoid at all costs as it's a tourist trap. The weather that day was very cooperative for Halloween in New York, and the camera crew took pictures of us all outside.

They allowed me to invite guests to attend the ceremony. In spite of the fact that my parents were out of town, Vina swooped in and filled the gap. And, boy, was I glad she was there! Then I asked folks that guided me along the way: people like Emo (my childhood friend), Nabil, Rob, and Will were alongside me amongst others.

Before the market close, the media crew gave us explicit instructions on the agenda. I was joined by Michael Capiraso, the President and CEO of New York Road Runners. He kicked things off before I read my prepared remarks. It was in that moment, reading those words live, that I realized I am driving something larger than I ever envisioned. The cameras were the only divider between me and the world.

I went out to dinner that evening at Manhattan Proper with a couple of buddies, and sifted through pictures from the events of that day. The donations continued to pour in, and when we broke $30K my heart was too full for my stomach to handle any food. I went to work the next day attempting to be coy, but my co-workers were not going to let me slip away from the flurry of questions. They were all incredibly supportive of the cause.

# A Thousand Reasons Why

NASDAQ had me on a high headed into race week. Even if you had no idea what it meant to ring the Closing Bell, the pictures served as enough indication that the campaign took a huge step forward. I had my head up knowing that everything played out well beyond my expectations. Everything was clicking; I couldn't ask for more.

My only concern going into that week was that I had little time to prepare for the actual race on Sunday. It was my first marathon, and I kept reminding myself, maybe I should focus less on the campaign and more on my body in anticipation of the main event.

The furthest I ran in training to that point was twenty-one miles. It was a beautiful run alongside the Hudson River from the bottom of Manhattan all the way up past the George Washington Bridge. It was as equally painful as it was scenic.

I convinced myself that, come Marathon Sunday, the adrenaline was going to carry me through. I also knew that, no matter what, I was going to finish that race; if not for myself, it would definitely be for my donors. After putting training concerns aside, my mind sprinted right back to $50K and how I could get us there by the end of the week. Sales has always been in my blood. Inherently I am driven by goals, and I measure myself daily on quotas. That $50K was now a quota. I had to get tactical; I was ready to share my story with anyone who would listen.

Three days before the event on November 2, I went to the Marathon Expo at the enormous Javitz Center on the west side of Manhattan. It was my first time at the Javitz, and I was overwhelmed by the size of the venue, the number of people it could hold, and the impressive ability of New York Road Runners to manage the flow of over 50,000 runners.

I went over to pick up my race bib. As is the case with most races, at the Expo different vendors were set up in throngs selling everything from running shoes to gels, to fitness trackers and energy drinks. I walked around, having no intention to buy anything. I just wanted to grab my bib and get back to the office.

As I went up and down the aisles, my mind was at work and a crazy idea popped into my head. I looked at my phone and pulled up the recent picture from NASDAQ. In a moment of boldness, I thought, "Maybe this is an opportunity for me to flip the script. Instead of purchasing products like everyone else, maybe I can impress a company by selling my story to the vendor."

I thought about Rob and Will, and how there was a reputational gain from partnering up with a positive message. If they would do it, it wouldn't be outrageous to take a shot.

I suddenly felt an adrenaline rush. I was going to do this. I didn't care if I got rejected; I had conviction in my plan. I then proceeded to walk back up to the front of the venue, and I made stops at each booth from one vendor to the next showing them my pictures from NASDAQ ringing the bell on TV. I shared with them the emails asking me to be a 'face of the marathon,' and proceed to tell them my story. I asked each vendor if they would consider getting behind my campaign in any capacity, and almost all of them passed on me politely.

I wasn't too surprised. I mean, who does that? I knew that was a real possibility and I was no less confident than I was when the day started. I would not be deterred, if anything I told myself it would be their loss. I kept going and walked over to the next vendor, it was Timex Sports, I asked if they had a marketing representative available and it happened to be that I was already speaking to him; his name was Keith.

Keith listened intently. He liked that I completed Eagleman because Timex is the official watch of Ironman. He stopped me before I could finish talking, and gave me GPS watches. He told me to auction them off. I obliged, and they generated donations immediately. He instructed me to stay in touch with him, and sent me more watches. My donor base was watching as I shared the story, and I received positive messages for thinking outside the box. I looked down at my watch, and realized I had taken a much-extended lunch break. I rushed back to the office. All I could think about that afternoon was going back to the Expo and hitting every single vendor that I had yet to get in front of.

That evening, as soon as I finished my work for the day, I rushed back to the Javitz Center. There was only a handful of vendors left. I was relieved, because I needed to go home and make dinner; I had not eaten all day. The first four vendors were quick rejections. I thought to myself I should be happy that Timex came on board, that was a flurry of donations I didn't expect. I could go home knowing I accomplished something extraordinary.

There was one last booth; it was the biggest in terms of square footage. The company was called Bedgear. I peeked in; it looked like a mattress company. I figured they would want nothing to do with me, but was a little curious as to why they were at a marathon expo.

Then I saw their tag line, "Sleep Fuels Everything." This was not your average bedding company; something was different. The booth was crowded with associates helping many customers on a restless night. I kept telling myself to walk away; I didn't want to waste my time waiting for someone to talk to.

As I was about to turn around, I caught the attention of a young lady. She was friendly, so I figured I had nothing to lose. I shared my story with her, and she listened intently. She pointed to a gentleman who was completing an interview with a reporter, and told me to sit tight as he would help me out.

I learned from her that Bedgear sold sleep performance systems. They encouraged people to reshape their views on how they sleep. The company thought of sleep as a chance to fuel up for the next day as opposed to resting off the last day. They had partnered up with major sports teams like the Dallas Mavericks and Boston Red Sox. I was shaking my head that I almost wrote them off as just another mattress company.

As I waited, I could tell the man looked swamped; I didn't want to be a nuisance. I asked the woman who had helped me if she was sure this was a good time. She said not to worry; he would be with me in a moment. He finished up his interview, walked up to me enthusiastically, and introduced himself as Eugene Alletto. Eugene told me that his daughter, Taylor, had shared my story with him. As the CEO of Bedgear, he wanted to make sure that my campaign received a full performance sleep system valued at nearly $3,000.

My jaw dropped. I was expecting a pillow, maybe a gift certificate. Never did I think I'd find myself talking to the CEO of the company. He told me that I was doing the right thing; he appreciated my hustle. That was a moment of affirmation, when my conviction was confirmed. If a complete stranger buys into your story, then you are doing something right. I went home that night with a total loss of appetite and an abundance of emotion.

*

The night after meeting Eugene, I couldn't sleep, I was too taken aback by his buy-in. I couldn't believe that my plan to solicit vendors actually worked. I momentarily thought again about how my body should be preparing for Sunday's race, that I should figure out a way to get some rest. But once again during this campaign, my emotions took over.

I kept thinking about how to learn from that day's experience, how I could potentially continue to push boundaries to catapult the campaign. I was all-in on achieving the goal of $50,000. I was ready to do whatever was necessary.

The following day, I was invited to take part in the Opening Ceremonies for the TCS New York City Marathon in Central Park right around the official finish line. The Ceremonies were to be covered live on ABC, and as a result of my fundraising and media success, I was invited by the Leukemia and Lymphoma Society to represent the organization alongside Ashton and Brianne Eaton who were invited that weekend as the organization's celebrity ambassadors. Since both were decorated Olympians, I made sure to do my homework. It was going to be a real privilege spending time with them, and I was looking forward to it. I made it over to the Park that afternoon and found my campaign manager, who guided me through the crowd and took me to the staging area.

Ashton and Brianne were chatting with folks from the Leukemia and Lymphoma Society, and once they finished up, I was introduced. I remember shaking Ashton's hand; it was like meeting an acquaintance. He was a record-holding Olympic Champion, but his approachability highlighted his humility. Brianne, who won a Bronze Medal in 2016, was very kind and it was delightful engaging with her. I could tell right away that they weren't being fake because they were 'on business.' They were genuinely modest people. I was instantly drawn to their energy. I didn't know how much time I'd get to spend with them. However, I made it a point to try and soak up anything I could. I knew they had something to offer.

We spent nearly a half-hour waiting for the events of the evening to begin, and we were in the middle of Central Park. I spoke with the two of them the entire time, learned about their background, and they shared some of their short-term plans. They were both about my age, so we had a lot in common except for the fact that I have no Olympic medals.

They had been briefed a little on my story, and I opened up with Ashton to fill him in on the crazy ride over the past couple months. I talked to him about the more recent momentum of my campaign, telling him about NASDAQ and Bedgear.

I was conscientious of throwing too much information at them; I didn't want to do all the talking. In fact, I was eager to listen to any insight the two might have regarding mental preparation for a big race, such as the TCS New York City Marathon. Simultaneously, in the back of my mind, I was burdened by the fact that I had to give a speech the following day at the National Blood Cancer Conference. I was seeking inspiration, yet I didn't know how to ask for it. I didn't know if it would be weird. We just met, and I didn't want to come off crazy.

After the ceremony was complete, we went to dinner at a local burger joint. There were many people from The Leukemia and Lymphoma Society with us that evening. I noticed that Ashton and Brianne stuck by me throughout the evening when they could have shuffled around. It was that reassurance they seemed to like me as well that pushed me to be direct.

"Ashton, can I ask you for a favor?" I said. He agreed. I told him that I was nervous because I had to prepare for a speech in front of a big audience the next day. I wanted to make sure my message would resonate, ensuring I'd capitalize on the platform.

I proceeded to ask him, "When you first made it out on the Olympic stage, when you were in front of the whole world, what was running through your mind?"

Without hesitation, he said, "All I kept thinking to myself was that there are thousands of reasons why I shouldn't be here." He proceeded to talk about how difficult it was to make it that far; how many other qualified athletes do not make it to that stage. He talked about how lucky he was to avoid injury, and anything else that could have gone miserably wrong on his quest.

He opened up, sharing his moments of vulnerability. As he spoke, he got me more and more fired up. He told me about how he kept thinking about the reasons he didn't deserve his success, and how it was all he could think about the first time he was in front of an Olympic audience. I went home that night, and I typed away feverishly. His ability to dig deep with me, to be raw in sharing his feelings, that was the inspiration I'd been seeking.

# The Comeback is Always Greater than the Setback

## 22

# The Spirit Within You

The National Blood Cancer Conference was in the afternoon on Saturday, the day before the marathon. Usually, it is an independent event; the only reason it was held that weekend was because of a marathon. So there were more attendees and a more significant buzz than usual.

I was unsure if I was going to be able to connect with my audience. I never presented in front of doctors and researchers. perhaps they were accustomed to a particular style that a banker couldn't sync up with. I suppressed my concern, reminding myself that we're all human. My message was always intended to relate to the masses.

I was given a couple of invitations. My sister was tied up that morning, and I knew that I absolutely needed familiar faces in the crowd, so I invited Farrell, Kenny, and Kenny's wife, Lakshmi. I was lucky they came. I looked around the room that afternoon; it was a few hundred people.

That morning I had spoken to my parents. They planned to be in their hotel room to watch the live recording. I had my speech ready to go on a sheet right in front of me, making extra sure not to spill anything on it. This was one presentation I couldn't afford to deliver on the cuff.

I was the last speaker on the schedule. There were plenty of presentations given before mine, and the majority had leaned toward research. Unless you were in the medical community, you were likely a little lost.

After the final researcher spoke, the screen displayed the fundraising leaderboard. To my surprise, someone had caught up to me. We shared the award for top fundraisers. I wasn't going to get competitive about it, since it was all for a good cause but, in the back of my mind, I knew I wasn't done yet.

I accepted my award and went back to my seat. The next two speakers shared their stories. Unfortunately, each of them were simply narrating their biographies. They had compelling stories, and kudos to anyone who gets in front of an audience that size, but I knew that, to stir an audience, you need to invigorate them. You need them to put themselves in your shoes. I found comfort in knowing that Ashton inspired me to do just that.

As I got on stage, my voice trembled, I thought of my parents watching in their hotel room. I didn't want them to hear any hesitation, so I summoned strength, and cleared my throat.

*People keep saying 'thank you' to me for being here and for my campaign, and I keep scratching my head, because quite honestly I believe I owe you the thanks. You gave me a platform that I never envisioned, and I am a firm believer that when given a platform, you better use it to shine a light, even if that light only reaches one person.*

*Yesterday, I had the pleasure of catching up with Ashton (Eaton) as we were walking to the parade and we briefly shared stories, I learned we're only a year apart in age and although we had far different journeys, (believe it or not, no Olympic medals hanging at my place) we shared some similar fundamentals. We agreed on the importance of failure in developing success, and we acknowledged the importance of setbacks.*

*Ashton shared with me that, when he made it to the Olympics, he would have recurring thoughts of the 'thousands of reasons' why he shouldn't be on that stage with that audience and those thoughts only provided fuel for his fire. Well, I stand before you here today, and I tell you there are 'thousands of reasons' why I shouldn't be on this stage and why, throughout this week, I shouldn't have been on a national stage. Those reasons have been the fuel that inspired my campaign slogan: #breakbarriers.*

*My setbacks did not define me, but instead, they dared me. They dared me to challenge convention, and they dared me to take leaps. Over 25 years ago, I was diagnosed with ALL at the young age of 3 years old, in Egypt, where I was born and where my parents were raised.*

*Upon learning my diagnosis, my parents acknowledged they had to immigrate to ensure my recovery. Leaving everything they knew in their twenties, they brought me to the City of Hope in California where I received treatment and, a year later, to North Shore in Long Island where I completed treatment.*

*The setbacks medically are pretty self-explanatory; however, the story is deeper than that. I was a child who just didn't fit in; I had to grow up quick in a landscape that was foreign to my family at the time. The language was a barrier; the culture was a barrier; the social setting was a barrier.*

*No matter what I did during my elementary and junior high years, I just couldn't click with my peers. On my thirteenth birthday, a year before I started high school, I had to have an intense brain surgery to remove a golf-ball-sized mass from the right frontal lobe of my brain. Something clicked for me after that experience, and after being in the hospital for several weeks, I was ready to take life into my own hands, and I wasn't going to let anyone hold me back.*

After all those years of treatment and surgery, with tubes coming out of places they shouldn't be for a child, I had more ammo to take on the real world than the majority of my peers. I was persuasive because I had grown up quick and I learned the importance of patience, understanding you may not see the results you want right away, but if you persist, you'll get to your destination.

It was that perspective that carried me when I wanted to make friends in high school. I wasn't just looking to make buddies; I was looking to stand out and be a name everyone knew. When I wanted to play sports and compete, even though the notion was that I would fail. After all that chemo, I was never going to be an athlete, and then I made the football team.

It was that perspective when a college counselor told me not to get my hopes up that I would work at an investment bank after college which allowed me to scratch and claw my way into the biggest bank in America. It was that perspective when I was told I'd be better suited working in a more analytical role, that I navigated myself into a front office seat.

It is that perspective which has carried me through 12 half marathons, 3 triathlons, and most recently a Half Ironman. It is that perspective that will guide me in navigating with a purpose once I cross that finish line on Sunday. It is that perspective that will allow me to focus my efforts on helping others going through these trials so they too can break barriers and know that no obstacle is too big. I've learned that the task ahead of you is not nearly near as grand as the spirit within you.

There are thousands of reasons why I should not be standing in front of you. I do not deserve the platform, but now that I'm here, I hope to use it for good. You should know this campaign almost didn't occur, and, boy, I am glad it did. In June of this year, I ran the Eagleman race in Maryland, a 70-mile trek across swimming, biking, and running. It was quite the experience, and there were a couple moments where I had to dig deeper than before looking for the energy to finish the race. It was in those moments that I started to question my 'why' and now I can look back and say that I needed to have those moments of digging to rally the strength of this campaign.

Anyway, after deciding to take on the New York City Marathon, my initial intent was to pay the minimum fundraising out of pocket and call it a day. I then started to re-think it, and I reminded myself of those moments and how I could make a difference if I get behind the right cause. I drafted my story, and I shared it with a mentor, I told him that I would set my goal at $3K, pretty convinced I'd be covering the majority of that tab.

He read my draft and looked at me and said, you better make that goal $100K. I told him that was crazy and I met him in the middle, thinking I'd be happy if we hit $10K. Today, I am proud to announce we raised over $35K and we're not done. Let me tell you how confident I am, two days ago at the expo, I went from one vendor to the other, pitching my story and flat out asked for sponsorship. I had two companies agree to work with me on the spot, and their donations are going to help us get closer to our goal. When a stranger buys into your story, you're doing something right, and that's why I'm not hesitant about accomplishing this mission.

I will leave you with this note, tomorrow you runners will exit your comfort zone, and it will be exhilarating, the strength within is immeasurable, the power of will is infinite, barriers can and will be broken. The comeback is always more significant than the setback.

Thank you and go team!

I walked off the stage to the only standing ovation of the night. I gave Ashton a huge hug, and I realized there was only one thing left for me to do that weekend: cross that finish line.

## 23

# New York City Marathon

The week leading up to race day was indeed an emotional rollercoaster. I had not a single regret about any of the events, and I would not have changed a thing. It dawned on me after I left the National Blood Cancer Conference that adrenaline would have to play a more prominent role the next day than I initially thought.

I did not sleep well the majority of the week. I didn't eat as I would have before other races. Lastly, my mind was not centered on the physical task ahead of me.

I was overcome by emotion through Eugene's actions and Ashton's advice. I wished my parents were there to see me pour out my feelings on stage and I thought about them the night before the race. I got back to my apartment that evening, and I dimmed the lights to set the tone for an early night. I filled up my water bottle, set all of my alarms, and picked up the closest book to read myself to sleep.

In the dark of night on Sunday, November 5, 2017, it was go-time. My alarm started ringing just before 4 AM, it was one of those mornings where I was consciously awake before it made a sound. I hadn't slept much the night before in spite of turning the lights off around 9 PM. The roads and highways around New York City were shut down, making way for runners to get to the start line at the Verrazano Bridge in Staten Island.

My mind was running from the minute I got out of bed. I wish I could say I was living in the moment, but I was all over the place. I had to triple check to make sure I remembered my phone, my ID, and my nutrition bars. I knew it was going to be a long day, and the last thing I cared for was a mishap like forgetting an essential.

Once I left my apartment to head up toward my bus, all I could think about was how I was going to propel the campaign to $50,000 and hit my goal. I was thinking about all of the positive messages I had received from supporters, and it weighed on me that the goal I had set for myself was no longer just an aspiration, but quite frankly it was now a responsibility.

Since it all happened so quickly in a matter of months, I began to question how I even got myself to engage so many people. I was trying to summon the source of all that energy. I was looking outside the window of the yellow cab, intently gazing into the dark hours of the early morning.

I again thought about my parents and how I wish they had been there to see it all happen from NASDAQ to the National Blood Cancer Conference. But heck, I never saw it coming myself, so I certainly wasn't upset at them for it. Ironically, the last thing that was on my mind that morning was that I was about to run my first marathon. I assured myself that nothing was going to stop me from crossing that finish line that day. They would have had to carry me off the course.

Since my story was selected for broadcast coverage, I got to ride in the VIP bus to Staten Island and the coordinator was giving me details regarding my segment in which I would run side-by-side with ABC Reporter, Amy Freeze. I was given access to the VIP tent that morning with Ashton and Brianne, and that made a *huge* difference in the grand scheme of things logistically. I was given access to heat, bathroom facilities, coffee, and breakfast. Although that might not sound like much, it was a way to ease the nerves before the race.

I felt terrible for the thousands of other runners, including my friends Kenny and Farrell. In the hours leading up the race, they were all scrambling for warmth and waiting on lines to relieve themselves. I was chowing down on bagels and Dunkin Donuts coffee next to a heater. Karlie Kloss, Tiki Barber, and Kevin Hart were among the celebrities in our tent. The cool thing about being in their company was that there was an understanding that stature would be insignificant. No matter how many cameras or reporters you had around you pre-race, running 26.2 miles was going to be humbling.

After completing my first interview with CBS, I was escorted back to the tent, and shortly after we proceeded toward the start line. As we were walking over, my mind again was in motion around fundraising. I made the quick decision to live record each mile marker to spur more donations throughout the race. Whatever it took I was hell-bent on $50,000.

Our tent was scheduled as one of the first corrals to kick things off. We lined up, and in the background, the speakers were blaring to Frank Sinatra's New York, New York. And it finally hit me that I was about to run perhaps the most incredible race in the world. I was going to run through all five boroughs of New York City, and I was going to do it in front of thousands of people.

I stared ahead at the Verrazano Bridge, took a deep breath, and any concerns I had about training subsided because the energy around me at that moment was just too damn positive to have the slightest doubt.

Michael Capiraso was set to kick things off for us at the podium overlooking the water. He congratulated us on making it out on what was shaping to be a beautiful day. He checked the road for security clearance and, before I knew it, the gun went off.

I had to maintain a relatively slow pace out of the gate because I was scheduled for my in-race interview at a specific mile-marker. I had to align my speed with the broadcast or else they might miss me. I'll admit that—even though I knew about the broadcast coverage beforehand—once I got going, my adrenaline levels were way out of sync. I had a ball of energy inside ready to burst. Eventually, I leveled down to my comfortable race pace.

Mentally, it felt like I was barreling through my fuel tank without hitting the proper distance points. I knew that was going to catch up to me. I pushed back on any doubts that crept in regarding my pace and kept running forward. Ashton ran with me for the first couple of miles until about Mile 7—where it was time for the interview—and that helped keep me focused.

The famous transition from Queens to Manhattan over the 59th Street Bridge is a mental block for many runners. It's the point in the race where you have a steep uphill run, and you witness people losing their stride coming over the bridge. As soon as you get off the bridge, however, you're welcomed by a loud roar from the Manhattan audience.

There were many moments on that bridge where I wanted to stop and take a breath, but Farrell's voice was in my head reminding me of the cardinal rule. I stopped peeking to the sides, so other runners wouldn't distract me. I kept my eyes ahead of me. Coming over that bridge, I started to acknowledge that I was going to accomplish this mission, and my sole objective at that point was to keep my mind in check.

I got off the bridge and made the turn on 2nd Avenue. The energy from the crowd shuttered any lapse in focus. New York fans are like no other, they don't have to know you personally to respect your grit, and upon exiting the bridge, I was in combat mode.

More than halfway through the race, my supporters were on my mind. In my pocket, my phone was blowing up with words of encouragement. I kept sharing updates at every mile, and we were inching toward $40,000 in funds raised. I was running alone physically at that point, but mentally, I knew that there were hundreds of people who had been following my progress.

There were moments around then where my legs weighed on me, but my supporters kept me going unbeknownst to them. I kept reminding myself that I owed it to them to show strength in moments of weakness.

*

As I was approaching the Bronx at Mile 20, my body wasn't just weighed down, it was in pain. My hips were sore. Every time my foot pounded the pavement, a sensation shot up through my entire body. It was alarming, but I refused to address it. I was approached on the course by coaches from the Leukemia and Lymphoma Society's running team. They had been tracking me and—after noticing that my stride was weakening—wanted to run by my side.

They asked me if I was okay, and probably knew that something was wrong, but I wouldn't relent no matter how painful things got. My mind was overpowering any physical pain, and I had no care to stop. I told them I was fine and that I'd push through. They understood and wished me well.

I kept pushing. Every step was more painful than the last. Shortly after I came around the corner for the last four miles in Central Park and, to my delight, the crowd was a factor once again. The greenery of the Park was a sign of life. It was at that moment, I realized that I was in new personal territory.

Guides will tell you that if you run twenty miles your body can handle twenty-six miles. Physically that's true, but mentally that new challenge can shock you. I should have remembered my first race, the Hamptons Half Marathon, when I had to push myself those last three miles because I had only trained for ten.

Your body has a not-so-subtle way of nudging you when you mark new territory in your mileage. I tried channeling Dyan, repeating "I Can, I Am, I Will" but this time it wasn't going to work.

A couple close friends of mine were spectating around Mile 24. I was borderline delirious by then, the pain was blinding. I started to see hints of salt on my skin that reminded me of Eagleman even though I purposely hydrated more than usual. As I ran toward the Mile 24 marker, I heard my name, but I was out of it. I missed a few people, front and center, cheering me on.

The unanimous feedback from them afterward was, "When we saw you, you didn't look good." The truth was that I did empty the tank earlier than I anticipated. That was likely due to the excess adrenaline I was trying to manage at the start of the race. By Mile 24, I was dragging my body. My mind was in a different universe.

At around Mile 25, I was desperate for motivation. Anything to push me for that last mile; anything so the pain could stop. I looked up and saw Karlie Kloss in the corner of my eye. I thought to myself, if only for the story, it'd be cool to cross the finish line side by side with a Victoria's Secret supermodel. I knew my buddies would appreciate it. I took a deep breath and dug into the tank.

I paced myself with Karlie's security crew (I had no such team). After about twelve minutes of keeping my eye on her bodyguard and trying to keep pace, I crossed that finish line. In storybook fashion, Ashton alongside a delegation from the Leukemia and Lymphoma Society, were waiting for me with my medal.

I immediately fell into his arms. I wasn't crying on the outside, but I was balling on the inside. I was overcome with emotion after fighting through the demons at Mile 20. I felt like I fulfilled my end of the promise to my donors and it meant everything to me that Ashton, a source of inspiration, was right there waiting for me.

My body took a beating that day. There was no hiding it. Every picture I took after the race was highlighted by a grimace. I don't have a single decent photo from the that day. A friend of mine, Nicole (unbeknownst to me) happened to be a finish line medic for the Marathon. It was like I had been sent an angel as she guided me to meet my sister at the exit. I could barely walk on my own. I was struggling to stand.

After the race, the plan was to go to Farrell's apartment and change before we headed out to celebrate at Proper West. Although his place was only a few blocks away from the finish line, the distance felt daunting. That difficult walk with Vina was rather intimate. I struggled mightily, and she pushed me to carry forward. Looking back, I realized that Vina had become my biggest fan. Perhaps the person who knows me best. Growing up, she never resented the fact that I got more attention as the firstborn, and that my circumstances drove many of my parents' decisions throughout our childhood.

In that moment, I acknowledged how blessed I was to have her in my corner. I realized that Vina witnessed my most vulnerable states, and she consistently projected an aura of strength and positivity during those difficult times. She has seen me stumble, fall, cry, give up on myself, give up on others, lose my poise at times, and yet she stood there beside me in spite of all my weakness. It may have only been a few blocks but, in recognizing all that, I found immense gratitude despite the pain I was feeling.

*

At Farrell's apartment, I got in the shower, and the hot water felt heavenly since I was aching everywhere. It was hands down the best shower I've had in my entire life. Putting my clothes back on was a struggle, but I knew that we had to get moving, and—if I sat down —I'd be done for the night.

I had no appetite after the race. As much as I wanted to celebrate, I couldn't stomach a beer or anything besides water. When we arrived, to my surprise, Rob and Will had catered a full spread for my group. I was overwhelmed with gratitude by their unceasing investment in my mission. A few months ago, these guys barely knew me, and suddenly they were like family.

I was exhausted, and I felt defeated physically, but I was thrilled to see many of the people who supported me along the way drop in that evening. It was a heartwarming moment where I realized that this campaign, and the medal around my neck, was by no means an individual accomplishment, but rather it was something we had undertaken as a community.

I did my best to enjoy the night in spite of the pain but I wasn't fully relaxed. I knew in the back of my mind there was still some work to be done. I was hovering at around $41,000 in funds raised. The race was over, but I was still kicking, I was going to get us across the finish line the same way I made it past Mile 20. I went home that night, I got in bed and fell asleep almost immediately, but the minute I woke up, I was thinking about only one thing, and that was simply to close the gap and hit $50K.

# Haley Strong

The morning after the marathon, I woke up again before my alarm. I slept well, but it was as if my mind had sent a memo to my body overnight that it wasn't time to get comfortable just yet; I was on alert. To my surprise, I wasn't very sore and thank goodness for that because I never planned to take off from work that day.

I got in the shower, and immediately I felt underwhelmed. No shower would ever be as refreshing as the one I took twelve hours prior after crossing the finish line. I proceeded to get dressed, and—as I was putting on my tie in front of the mirror—I acknowledged that, for the first time in weeks, it was back to the old routine.

I had a moment of internal conflict. In those weeks of training, every day I got out of bed feeling a tremendous sense of purpose. Now here I was donning my suit for 'another day at the office.'

It was a Monday morning, and I arrived at work just before a weekly meeting at 8 AM. The room was crowded room, as usual. After about a half-hour, the moderator gave a quick nod to the runners from the day before. At that moment, I felt my legs starting to lock up from sitting. I proceeded up the elevator to my desk on the 23rd floor. On the way over, I was stopped by a couple of my colleagues who congratulated me and said I looked good on TV. I took a step back. I was so beat up in those last six miles of the race that I completely forgot I had recorded a segment; it felt like ages ago. I went over to my desk, and before I started to dig into my work for the day, I emailed the New York Road Runners PR rep to request a copy of the taping.

Throughout the day, I received random messages congratulating me, ranging from senior management to my peers. I smiled and said 'thank you' numerous times, but deep down I felt that—by accepting their kind messages—I needed to keep the mission alive, though I had no idea how. I simply knew it wasn't dead.

Over the next few days, I shared pictures and videos on social media recapping the journey my supporters and I had been on. When I mentioned that the page would remain open, I saw a sprinkling of donations come in. We were inching closer to $45K. At that point, I accepted that closing the gap was going to be a game of inches, small donations here and there. Hopefully, we'd get to a place close enough that someone could get us across the goal line.

Before this campaign, I was no social media wizard. Admittedly, I'm still not. I don't really implement much of a strategy. In fact, I'm probably more impulsive then I should be when it comes to hitting the 'share' button. However, I did learn one thing during the weeks after the race: content draws appeal. I knew I had material to give; I just wasn't sure where to give it.

In early December, I was invited to a networking event at The Muse Headquarters in Midtown. It was a random invite, actually. I don't usually respond to those, but I had been following The Muse for a long time. I was a big fan of their material. The Muse is a content-rich site directed toward millennials, offering up career advice, helping their readers seek out professional advancement. I was unsure what my purpose was that night, I didn't have much of an interest in working in that industry, but I knew they shared material that applied to people across generations navigating their careers.

When the event started, we all gave quick introductions and shared our professions. I was the only one there coming from a bank, and that led to a number of routine questions, like "Aren't the hours crazy?" and "Do you have to wear a suit every day?" I tried to change the subject; I didn't want to talk about my day job. That wasn't the reason I was there.

After the general session, I started speaking to a young lady who asked me what I liked about The Muse and what drew me to the event. I said I enjoyed the authenticity of their articles. The advice they gave to young professionals wasn't cliché, it felt personal. She nodded and said that's undoubtedly a focus for them; it's probably what separated them from the pack.

She talked to me about The Muse in general and the direction they were moving in terms of growth and strategy. Her vision really appealed to me. I asked her if they wrote all their pieces in-house or if they worked with outsiders. She smirked.

"Why?" she asked, "Do you want to write something for us?" There I was buttoned up in my suit, and I bashfully said, "Yeah, kind of I think I have something."

She inched a little closer to listen to what I had to say. There I was giving my elevator pitch on the fly for the first time.

"I work in finance," I said, "and while it may seem like roses to an outsider, I have something else that could suit your audience. I have a story to share around navigating unemployment."

Bingo. I had her roped in. I walked her through my journey from college to JP Morgan, and gave an abbreviated version of the course of events since then. I said my article would translate the lessons learned battling cancer to success in the workplace.

"Send me a write-up as soon as possible," she smiled. "I'll be happy to review it."

I didn't waste a moment. I got home that evening and, all of a sudden, the momentum of the campaign came rushing back. I had a draft sent to her before I went to bed. The next day she responded and gave me the thumbs up. The Muse was willing to work with me. Just like that, I was going to have my first article published. I was back in the game in terms of content to share.

That got me thinking, "Why stop there?" I reached out to City of Hope, telling them I wanted to write an article for their publication. They accepted right away. I was on a roll. I was confident these articles would help me keep the spirit of the campaign alive. I acknowledged that it was unusual for someone to continue fundraising after an event, but I suppressed negativity; the message was worth any awkwardness I might feel.

*

About a month later, I arrived at work and, to my surprise, received an email from a client. The subject read: "Haley Strong."

> *Good Morning, Bishoy,*
> *Thanks for the updates and I wanted to congratulate you on your charity successes! I get your updates, and it makes me happy to see you thriving for your cause.*
> *Yesterday, I dropped off a little something for a 3-year-old girl who was recently diagnosed with Leukemia. Her name is Haley, and she is the daughter of a CrossFit coach I met two times here in CT. Haley is just beginning her fight, and I went out of my way to ensure I helped her family during the initial diagnosis stage of their new lives.*

I read that, and was blown away. Let me put this in perspective for you. I knew that my campaign had reached a broad audience, and my donor base was more extensive than I ever imagined. But I had only interacted with this client a handful of times, so he owed me nothing. This, however, was more important than any donation;

this was practically a stranger who was moved to pay it forward and help someone in need. It was my mission in action.

I shared his note with my follower base, and more donations came in. In the weeks after, I was invited to kick off the winter training season for the Leukemia and Lymphoma Society's team. When asked to speak, I read the message reminding everyone in the room that ultimately this is what it's about.

I knew that $50,000 was only a matter of time at this point, but I was mindful of how and when I would ask donors. I took a few weeks for my body to recover after the marathon. I had suffered a minor sprain, so I needed to take a step back from training. It was mentally taxing for me to give up my mornings at Swerve; I needed my TEAM at that time as I navigated my next steps.

Once I got the green light to start training again, I headed back to the studio, and picked up where I left off. It just so happened that my TEAM was mapping out their next undertaking and, of course, they wanted to get me on board. But I couldn't commit to anything until I accomplished what I set out for originally.

During that conversation, one of the women, Sarah, suggested I should consider speaking, particularly since I'd been writing so many pieces. She worked at a major investment bank and thought there might be an opportunity for me.

"Who me?" I thought. "A major company out there wants to pay me to speak?" I'm not shy around a microphone or on stage; I'm not intimidated by public speaking. Nonetheless, I never imagined that a door like that would open for me.

I spent the next few weeks finalizing the arrangement. I still couldn't believe I was going to get paid for talking primarily about my life. I worried how this would be perceived by my management at JP Morgan. I didn't want anyone to think that I was venturing off into public speaking because, quite frankly, I didn't know if I was good enough. For all I knew, this was a one-off.

I put together a slide deck around 'Break Barriers', intending to discuss how one can translate success in fundraising to success in a sales organization. I practiced over and over, rehearsing in front of audiences beforehand. I calmed my nerves the only way I knew how, I called my father for advice (remember, he speaks to a live audience on a weekly basis). He reminded me that, when it comes to being a storyteller, it's all about leveling with your audience— never to talk *at* them, take them with you on your journey.

As the day approached, I reached out to Amy Freeze, and I invited her to kick things off. At that point, she had covered the TCS New York City Marathon for ABC for a couple years. She has seen firsthand the impact of several other stories. I also invited Bedgear, Swerve, and the NIEUW Group to partake as a way to show the audience that—although it all started with me as an immigrant child navigating obstacles—ultimately the comeback was never about just me. It was about the people who empowered me to share my message.

The bank made a kind donation, which brought us to nearly $48K. People on the outside took note that I was keeping this thing alive, another round of donations came in. By happenstance, the founder of another small business, Time Tailored, was in the room, as well. He immediately pledged support.

After a successful delivery that day, I thought that, from an optics perspective, it was a little off that I was paid to speak at a competitor and client of JP Morgan. I figured I should reach out to our communications team to let them know. I set up a meeting and was very direct. I told them my story. I showed them the articles and the media coverage. I said that I had spoken at this other bank, and thought that they should be looped in.

A few days later, I got an email from an editor of our internal newsletter. She wanted to connect and put together a story. She told me that this was not the norm. In fact, features like what she was considering are reserved for members of the operating committee.

We met, and I gave her the background. She asked if I'd be willing to speak at the firm-sponsored Cycle for Survival event that month. I said I'd love to. The week after the event, the article came out; my inbox was flooded with kind messages. Folks were asking me to send them the donation link. I was getting donations from people I had never met.

A day later, I got the email I never saw coming. It was from Mary Erdoes, the CEO of JP Morgan Asset Management. She congratulated me on the article and the success of the campaign. I replied boldly, asking if I could have five minutes of her time. I wanted to let her know that, had it not been for a senior leader named Tim, the campaign would never have happened.

Well, before I said that, Mary asked me to speak at her weekly meeting to all of JP Morgan Asset Management. Note that her meeting is attended and led by the most senior representatives of the firm. It features the lead economists and portfolio managers, the same personalities seen on CNBC. Everyone in the organization attends or listens in. If I were anything short of above average, this appearance could break my career. I had only three days to prepare, so I worked with the communications staff to hone my message.

That Monday morning, I was up there alongside Mary and other senior leaders. I was scheduled to speak during the last part of the agenda. When it came time, Mary set the stage for me; she had a way with words. She mentioned that my story was a good reminder to the firm that we needed to keep things in perspective. We needed to maintain a balance between our purpose in day-to-day activities versus the bigger picture and our deeper call for fulfillment.

Her introduction was perfect, so my part was easy. I recapped my mission, but most importantly I told the audience that it all started within the walls of the institution. I encouraged folks to seek out mentors like mine (Tim) who would push them to aim high.

On April 6, 2018, nearly five months after the TCS NYC Marathon, I received an anonymous donation that put us over the top. Words wouldn't do the feeling I had any justice. Nearly $10,000 was raised after the race, and opportunities to continue sharing the message kept sprouting from various directions.

# Postscript

Nearly a year later, I was invited by New York Road Runners to speak to charitable organizations looking to take part in the next TCS NYC Marathon. I reminded the audience that they are giving people a platform to share their most personal stories, a unique arena to connect with others.

I shared with them how I was not a marathon runner; I had no intent to fundraise; I barely knew the charity I linked up with. All I wanted was to inspire someone to believe that barriers are meant to be broken. I talked about the shift from aspiring to hit $50,000 to feeling a sense of responsibility. I encouraged them to work with their champions to take advantage of the platform in a way where everyone can come out a winner.

I found in writing this book the hardest part was knowing when I was done. The fact of the matter is I've realized again and again that my story is far from over. I was recently invited up to Geneseo to speak to students about channeling the mindset to overcome obstacles.

I was asked the question, "If you could go back ten years and give younger Bishoy a piece of advice, what would you tell him?" I responded honestly, "Life is not nearly as mapped out as you think it is; the detours are the most important part."

I reminded them of the moment the career counselor told me that I should re-think my course. I talked about how I applied the lessons I learned throughout my life to turn a perceived roadblock into an opportunity.

I would ask you to take a moment to reflect on your 'why' and then consider sharing your story. In an age where you can't hide much because of social media, the onus is on us to use that visibility for good. Looking back, my twenties were a whirlwind. I was overly confident about my prospects in various areas of my life even though I was surrounded by uncertainty.

On the outside, I felt unstoppable. I had great friends; I was healthy; I never shied away from pursuing relationship, both personal and professional; and I always shoot my shot (see emailing Mary Erdoes). At the end of the day, I figure I've been let down with enough bad news for a lifetime. What's a rejection going to do beyond strengthen and teach me to get back up? Like I tell folks: "Embrace the fall, because it always precedes the rise."

On the inside, I was less secure. I knew I wasn't where I wanted to be in terms of employment. I faced an uphill battle in my ambition to join the ranks on Wall Street, since was I graduating from a small state school in western New York during the worst financial crisis in over seventy years.

It all began to come together, however, under the guidance of exemplary mentorships, and when I pushed myself out of my comfort zone at Mile 40. That's when I realized enough is enough; it was my purpose to share the principles behind my drive—to always seek out opportunity in moments of darkness, display patience, maintain perspective, and keep your head up knowing that the comeback is *always* greater than the setback.

# Acknowledgments

**Mom and Dad**

You set the stage when you decided to take the leap and leave your home as young newlyweds with an entire lifetime ahead. You left a future of stability, depicted by the neighborhoods you grew up in, and the culture that had been ingrained within you. You left your families who stood by you, and your lifetime friends, to enter the unknown of a new country. You stared down the challenges ahead accepting that it was your only choice.

Little did you know that, although life felt like a movie with one twist after another, your willingness to take on discomfort would lay the foundation for everything that would abound from there. You consistently leaned on your faith, your instincts, and your community.

As a result, your example has instilled confidence within me to follow my own intuition, a determination to exude resilience in dark times, and an unwavering focus on moving forward in the face of obstacles. You taught me how to play the game of life with the cards as they've been dealt. I am forever grateful to you both for your unconditional support.

## Vina

I am incredibly proud of the person you are, and I'm joyed by the bond that we've built as siblings and friends. You have been there through it all, the highs and the lows. You've seen me at my most vulnerable moments, and you helped keep my head above water when I was ready to give up.

You are always thoughtful in your advice, and your kindness is reflected in all of our interactions. Thank you for being a real example of a person unafraid to pursue their dreams.

In watching your journey, I've gleamed with pride, and I've also picked up inspiration to tackle projects such as my fundraising initiative and this book. I'm very appreciative of all the time that you have spent to help me share this message, and for your investment in guiding me to put the best product forward.

## Tim Kenrick

My entire life I felt as though I had a story to share and, for nearly thirty years, I kept it inside. I hesitated up until the final moment, nervous that what I thought was impactful to me may not resonate with others. Then, like an angel out of nowhere, you became the mentor that I was seeking.

It was 2017 on a July afternoon in that 23rd–floor conference room where you gave me the push that I had sought my entire adult life. Without your positive spirit, your faith in my ability to lead, and your conviction in my message, this story never would have been told.

You taught me to dream big, to never waiver in pursuit of greatness, to always keep my head up high, and to encourage those around me. Thank you from the bottom of my heart for believing in me when I was hesitant to believe in myself. As far as I am concerned, you are the epitome of authentic leadership, your selfness, your humility, and your energy lit a spark within me that will remain until the day my journey ends. I aspire to one day be that light to someone else.

### Nabil Fahmy

From the very first day we met, you took me in as your own son. You did not know me; you knew little of my beginnings, and yet you trusted me. You gave me the guidance to succeed in a city that is relentless in its demands. You taught me how to stand out from my peers, and you kept me grounded when I was ready to give up.

I was genuinely undeserving of your consideration. I stumbled at times, and you believed I would get up. Because of that, I refused to stay down.

### Kenny Zawistowski and Farrell Denby

I love my sister, but I've always thought about how life would have been with a brother. I never considered that I'd end up having two, and that I'd meet them both at the same time. Fortunately for me, you both embody similar positive qualities. It's been a privilege sharing years of experiences together.

As brothers you have been loyal to the highest degree. You've exemplified determination, and you've given me the feedback I needed in moments when I was blinded. You are open, honest, and courteous in your delivery. I've always felt reassured that you have my best interest in mind.

You've sometimes proven to know me better than I know myself, and I'm thankful for the protection that your bond has highlighted. Thank you both for being the first to preview this book and for your selfless involvement in its release.

### Michael Ervolina (Ervo)

No other way I would have the story play out. You showed up at a time when my tank was empty; you helped me in a period where I nearly lost hope. You didn't hesitate, and you weren't deterred by my lack of experience. Your faith in me helped me uncover the potential to knock down walls throughout my career, and I'll carry that with me forever. Thank you for passing along that resume, for taking me under your wing, and for taking a shot on me when you really didn't have to.

### Rob Zahn and Will Strozier
Your unwavering support, your endless encouragement, and your genuine investment in my mission have given me an exceptional sense of reassurance. You taught me that the sky is the limit when it comes to spreading a message of empowerment.

When I think about community, I think about you and your actions. You lifted me up, and I hope to return the favor one day. I am proud to say I know you, and I am excited about your future prosperity. Thank you to the entire Proper family for welcoming me and joining me on this mission.

### Michael Capiraso and the NYRR family
As you've heard me tell others, the NYC Marathon gave me a platform that I never envisioned, and I cannot correctly express the sense of responsibility and purpose that came along with that stage. I am grateful for your partnership, for your trust, and for all that you do for those who have stories to tell.

### WOLACO
Upon completing *Break Barriers*, it became evident to me, more than ever, that this story was about my broader circle of influence. I found strong alignment with your commitment to community and your dedication to always being better than you were yesterday.

Thank you to the entire WOLACO family for graciously allowing me to be an ambassador for not only your brand but, more importantly, your mission.

*

A most sincere thank you to all of the friends and extended family who have supported me and my family as we weathered the storms of treatment and hospital stays. A warm sentiment of gratitude to Emo and George for your bond of friendship and investment in my mission.

# Author Bio

Bishoy Tadros is a sales professional in New York City. As a young child, and an immigrant from Egypt, he battled with acute lymphoblastic leukemia. That experience helped him to develop a mindset of overcoming obstacles. From that basis, Bishoy created a playbook to navigate his career in the heart of the financial crisis, embracing all the challenges that came in his path.

He talks about the application of those lessons to his fitness goals, such as completing a grueling Half Ironman. In 2017, Bishoy undertook the TCS New York City Marathon and raised over $50,000 for The Leukemia and Lymphoma Society.

Bishoy's story is universal. It's about learning to apply the virtues of patience, perspective, and purpose to achieve whatever you dream in life. He draws a parallel between the success he came upon sharing his message of hope, and the application of that message personally, professionally, and on the the playing field.

Made in the USA
Middletown, DE
14 July 2020

12825284R00106